The Sewing Stitch
and Textile Bible

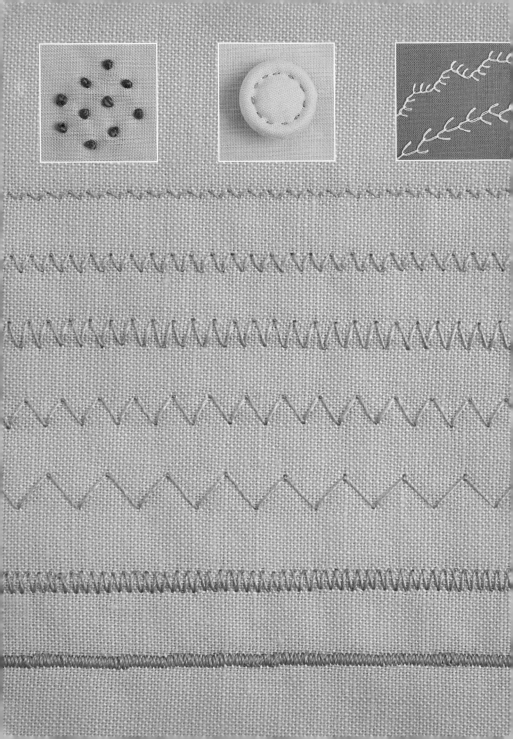

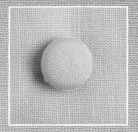

The Sewing Stitch and Textile Bible

An illustrated guide to techniques and materials

LORNA KNIGHT

CHARTWELL
BOOKS, INC.

A QUARTO BOOK

This edition published in 2013 by
Chartwell Books, Inc.
A division of Book Sales, Inc.
276 Fifth Avenue, Suite 206
New York, New York 10001
USA

ISBN: 978-0-7858-3035-1

QUAR.TSSB

Conceived, designed, and produced by
Quarto Publishing plc
The Old Brewery
6 Blundell Street
London N7 9BH

Project editors Mary Groom & Katie Hallam
Art editor and designer Julie Francis
Managing art editor Anna Plucinska
Assistant art director Caroline Guest
Copy editor Sue Viccars
Illustrator Kuo Kang Chen
Photographer Phil Wilkins
Proofreader Diana Chambers
Indexer Dorothy Frame

Art director Moira Clinch
Publisher Paul Carslake

Color separation by Modern Age
Printed in China by Midas Printing International Ltd.

Contents

Introduction

I have been sewing for as long as I can remember, starting with dolls' clothes made from offcuts from my mother's sewing box. When I was a teenager I made clothes for myself. As I grew older I wanted new challenges and moved toward tailoring, lingerie, and bra making. I firmly believe that there is always more to learn, especially with newly developed fabrics and ever-improving technology in sewing machines.

I hope this book will confirm your confidence in your sewing and introduce you to new techniques that will enable you to sew quicker and better than you do already. I hope you will find it an invaluable aid to your work.

Lorna

Stitch Directory

The Stitch Directory lists both functional and decorative stitches carried out by hand, sewing machine, and serger.

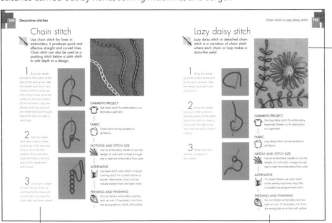

SAMPLE PHOTOGRAPH
The sample photographs show a finished example of the stitch, seam, hem, or fastening. Reverse photographs and enlarged details are shown when necessary.

STEP-BY-STEP INSTRUCTIONS
Follow the diagrams and instructions to help you perfect new stitches and techniques.

SPECIFIC ADVICE
Stitch details, garment/project advice, and fabric selection are given. Advice on suitable alternatives and pressing/ finishing details are also provided.

Techniques and Applications

This section offers step-by-step information on
how to create the best finishes.

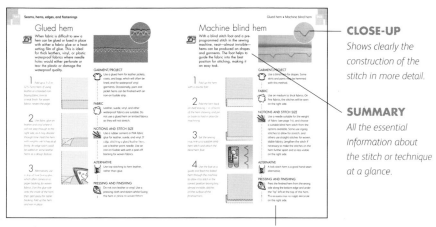

CLOSE-UP
*Shows clearly the
construction of the
stitch in more detail.*

SUMMARY
*All the essential
Information about
the stitch or technique
at a glance.*

Textile Directory

The Textile Directory is intended to give advice on
getting the best from different fabrics, including
choosing the most appropriate needles and seams.

INFORMATION PANEL
*Everything you need to know to apply
the stitch or technique correctly.*

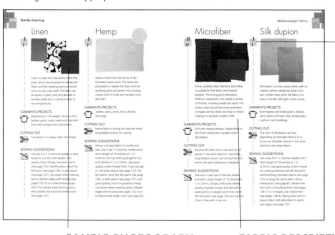

SKILL LEVEL
*An indication of skill
level is provided to
encourage beginners
and to serve as a guide
for skill development.*

SAMPLE PHOTOGRAPH
*The sample photograph shows an
example or examples of the fabric.*

FABRIC DESCRIPTION
*A fabric description is included to help in sourcing
suitable cloth for sewing particular garments and
projects. Names may vary but the description will
aid an appropriate selection.*

Tools and Equipment

As with any project, a task is so much easier if you use the correct tools. Having the right pair of scissors for each cutting task or the best needle for the chosen fabric will make sewing quicker and easier, as well as giving a better finish.

Getting started

The following items are essential for your sewing kit. They are readily available in all good sewing/haberdashery stores and are inexpensive to buy. Once bought, you'll use them time and time again.

Measuring tools

To ensure a good fit when making garments it is essential to work accurately with good quality measuring tools. Whether measuring long lengths of fabric or folding up a narrow hem, there is a tool for the job.

1 TAPE MEASURE

Choose a good quality tape measure that will neither ravel nor stretch. It should be at least 60 in. (150cm) long with clear measurements marked accurately from the start of the tape.

2 YARD (METER) STICK

Made of wood or metal, a stick is ideal for measuring lengths of fabric from a roll. The stable nature of a yard (meter) stick is also helpful when cutting fabric for drapes or shades.

3 MEASUREMENT GAUGE

This handy gadget allows small measurements to be checked easily. It is marked on both sides and is easy to manipulate when folding up hems, marking buttonholes, and positioning top stitching.

4 RULER

A 6 in. (15cm) ruler is useful when measuring drape hems or deeper hems on a skirt or dress. As it is solid and flat, it can lie on top of the folded hem and can be easier to handle than a tape measure.

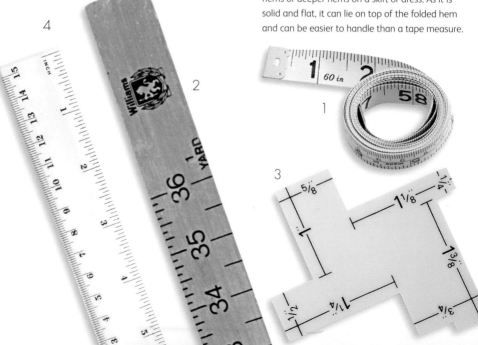

Marking tools

It is important to transfer pattern markings on to fabric pieces to position darts and pockets accurately. It also ensures a good fit when a garment is completed. Tailor's tacks can be sewn to mark important positions but chalks and pens are quicker to use.

5 CHALK

Chalk is a traditional material for marking cloth and can be brushed away when finished with. Chalk comes in triangular pieces, rollers, and pencils in various colors. Keep the edges or points sharp, mark on the wrong side of the fabric, and use a color which shows up well.

6 WASH-AWAY PENS

The ink from these pens (normally blue) can be wiped off with a damp cloth when finished with. It is advisable to try it out on a scrap of fabric first to check that the wetting doesn't damage it.

7 FADE-AWAY PENS

The ink from these pens (normally pink) will fade from the fabric within 48 hours. Check the pen on a scrap of fabric first to see whether it shows up on the chosen cloth and then disappears.

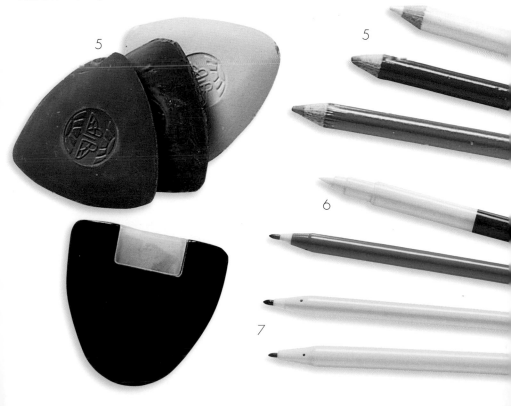

Cutting tools

There is a variety of cutting tools and scissors which make sewing tasks easier. Choose good quality scissors and tools and look after them, sharpening or replacing them when necessary.

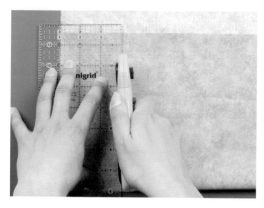

A rotary cutter enables accuracy, so it's ideal for cutting small fabric pieces and patterns.

SHEARS

Sharp, long-bladed scissors are ideal for cutting fabric quickly and with a smooth edge. Use these when cutting out fabric pieces, and cut drape lengths with long sweeping cuts. Make sure they are comfortable. Soft-handled shears are available.

1 PINKING SHEARS

Pinking shears have notched teeth which leave a zigzag edge to the cut cloth. This makes the fabric less likely to ravel. They are also ideal for craft work.

2 SERRATED SHEARS

These are occasionally useful if cutting thin, lightweight, soft fabric as the blades grip the fabric better and so it does not "run away" from the blades.

3 PAPER SCISSORS

It is essential to have a pair of scissors kept just for paper. Using fabric shears for cutting paper patterns will cause them to become blunt and useless for their intended task. They do not need sharp points but must cut paper cleanly.

4 NEEDLEWORK/EMBROIDERY SCISSORS

Scissors with short blades and sharp points are very useful. The sharp points can be used for cutting individual stitches or for getting into difficult-to-access corners for trimming. Use them for cutting threads and also for cutting the backing of synthetic fur fabric to avoid cutting the fibers.

5 ROTARY CUTTER AND MAT

A rotary cutter is very useful for cutting out small- to medium-sized pieces of fabric. It must be used in conjunction with a self-healing mat to protect both the working surface and the rotary blade. Buy the largest mat available and replace the rotary blades when necessary.

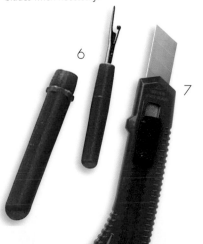

6 QUICK UN-PICK

A quick un-pick or a stitch ripper is useful when removing stitching. Cut every third stitch on one side, then turn the seam over and pull out the thread from the other side. Use it to open buttonholes: place a pin across one end and cut from the other end up to the pin.

7 CRAFT KNIFE

A small, sharp blade—used with care—is a useful tool for cutting leather and fur.

Ironing and pressing tools

An iron is an essential aid when sewing. It helps to hold the fabric in place and gives a crisp finish when required.

Dry iron
A dry iron can be used in conjunction with a damp cloth or water bottle spray when required. Some fabrics are damaged by water spots leaving permanent marks on cloth.

Steam iron
A steam iron contains a small tank of water and pushes steam through the cloth whilst ironing to improve its efficiency.

Tank iron
A tank iron has a large reservoir of water connected by a pipe to the iron. This type of iron produces a greater pressure of steam.

Pressing cloths
Pieces of cotton muslin and silk organza are perfect to protect the surface of fabric from the heat of the iron.

Pins and needles

Using the correct pins and needles can save hours of frustration. Pins can fall out of loosely woven fabric or damage threads on fine tightly woven cloth. Hand needles can be difficult to thread if the eye is too small, or can lose the thread if the eye is too large. The wrong machine needle can lead to skipped stitches, pulled threads, or can even break under the strain.

5

Dressmaking pins

These general-purpose pins are suitable for mediumweight fabrics and many tasks. They are especially useful when working on paper patterns or when pattern drafting.

1 GLASS-HEADED/PEARL-HEADED PINS

These are useful for most sewing projects with the advantage that if they are dropped on the floor they can be easily seen and picked up. They are also less likely to fall out of loosely woven cloth. Take care if the head of the pin is plastic as this will melt under the heat of the iron.

2 BRIDAL PINS

Bridal pins are especially long and fine to limit the damage to delicate fabrics.

3 QUILTER'S PINS

These very long pins are ideal for quilting.

4 FLOWER-HEAD PINS

These long pins with large, flat heads are ideal for loosely structured fabrics like lace, net, or tulle as they do not fall out.

5 SAFETY PINS

Use safety pins when ordinary pins are likely to fall out or are to remain in a project for some time. They are useful when sewing with net or tulle and also when quilting.

6 WEIGHTS

Use weights instead when a fabric could be damaged by pins. These can be fabric weights or kitchen weights if necessary. A house brick placed in a woolen sock is also useful.

Hand needles

There are many different hand needles available to suit the task, the cloth, and the thread being used. Choose the best needle in a suitable size.

7 SHARPS

These are fine, medium-length needles with small eyes for general sewing.

8 BETWEENS

Betweens are small, very fine needles with small eyes for fine sewing and small stitching.

9 EMBROIDERY NEEDLES

These are sharp needles with large eyes to take embroidery floss.

10 TAPESTRY NEEDLES

Tapestry needles are chunky with large eyes to take wool or thick thread and have rounded points to avoid splitting the threads of the cloth.

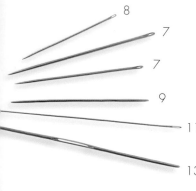

8

7

7

9

11

13

11 BEADING NEEDLES

These long, extra-fine needles will pass through the holes in beads.

12 BODKINS

Bodkins are large, blunt needles designed to thread elastic or cord through casings.

13 TWIN-POINTED

Twin-pointed needles have a hole in the center and two pointed ends. They are used for quick tapestry and chain stitch sewing.

Machine needles

Machine needles are now available to suit most types of fabric.

14 STANDARD/ UNIVERSAL

These are used for general stitching and many sewing tasks. The point is sharp enough to pierce woven fabric and round enough to push between the yarns of knitted cloth.

15 MICROTEX

Use Microtex needles for silks and microfiber fabrics. The sharp point penetrates woven fabrics.

16 BALL POINT

Ball point needles are designed for knitted fabrics. The needle pushes between the yarns of the cloth rather than splitting them.

17 STRETCH

Use stretch needles for knitted fabric which contains spandex (Lycra). The "scarf" (indentation at the back, just above the eye) is deeper on a stretch needle to catch the bobbin thread and prevent skipped stitches.

18 JEANS

Jeans needles are strong with a sharp point to penetrate heavy, thick fabrics like denim, canvas, or upholstery cloth.

19 TOP STITCH NEEDLES

Top stitch needles have larger eyes and grooves than standard needles. The eye is big enough to take two strands of ordinary thread or top stitching, button hole, or machine embroidery floss.

20 EMBROIDERY

Similar to top stitch needles, these have a large eye and special "scarf" (indentation at the back, just above the eye) to prevent the thread from being shredded.

21 METALLICA

A metallica needle is similar to an embroidery needle that is designed specifically for metallic threads.

22 LEATHER

A leather needle has a sharp point that cuts into leather or suede as it sews.

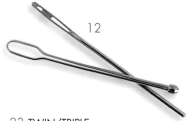

23 TWIN/TRIPLE

A twin or triple needle has two or three needles on a bar and on one shaft. It allows two or three parallel rows of stitching to be sewn at once.

24 WING

A wing needle has two broad wings on either side of the shaft. As the needle penetrates the cloth, the wings push the threads of the fabric apart and the stitch leaves an open hole. It creates heirloom or antique stitching.

25 QUILTING

A quilting needle has a longer, sharper point to stitch through several layers.

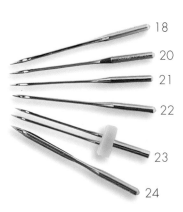

Tools and equipment

Sewing machines and sergers/overlockers

The sewer's biggest and most important investment is a sewing machine, and a serger follows closely behind. Both will give a neat, manufactured finish.

Sewing machines

Today's modern sewing machines are very different from those hand-powered, straight-stitch machines our mothers used. Computer technology now allows for numerous stitches to be pre-programmed, making functional, decorative, and embroidery stitching very simple. Although machines and models vary, they all work in the same basic way.

1 **BOBBIN WINDER** This winds the thread speedily and evenly on to the bobbin.

2 **THREAD SPINDLE** This may be horizontal or vertical and holds the reel of thread.

3 **THREAD GUIDES** These hold the threads in the correct route before reaching the needle.

4 **NEEDLE** This is held in place with a screw for easy changing.

5 **BOBBIN HOLDER** The bobbin is placed in its holder under the throat plate. It releases the thread under tension, allowing the thread to link with the needle thread to form a stitch.

6 **THROAT PLATE** This surrounds the feed dogs and covers the bobbin and bobbin holder, forming a flat surface. The needle travels down through the throat plate to pick up the bobbin thread below.

7 **PRESSER FOOT** The presser foot is lowered to hold the fabric in position while stitches are formed.

8 **FEED DOGS** The "teeth" grab the fabric and move it according to the length of stitch required.

9 **STITCH SELECTION** Buttons, dials, or a touch-sensitive screen allow selection of the stitch required.

10 **FLY WHEEL** The fly wheel or balance wheel can be turned by hand to raise or lower the needle.

11 **PEDAL** The foot pedal operates the machine at an appropriate speed. Sometimes an on/off button and a sliding switch on the machine will do this too.

Sergers/overlockers

These have become very popular in recent years as they allow home sewers to benefit from a manufactured seam finish. They also produce wonderful creative seams and edges, and sew modern stretch fabrics with ease.

1 THREAD SPINDLES

There are four of these on most sergers. The two on the left feed the needles and the two on the right feed the loopers.

2 THREAD GUIDES

These hold the threads in the correct routes before reaching the needles and loopers.

3 TENSION DIALS

These allow the threads to be adjusted and so form different types of stitch, for example, a balanced stitch, flatlocking, and rolled hemming.

4 NEEDLES

There are normally two needles on a serger. They may both be used for four-thread serging. Wide three-thread serging is made with the left needle in position. Narrow serging uses the right needle only.

5 LOOPERS

The loopers feed the threads below the needles and allow stitches to be formed when they link with the needle threads.

6 KNIVES

The knives cut off the excess fabric before the threads form stitches over the cut edge.

7 FLY WHEEL

The fly wheel or balance wheel can be turned by hand to raise or lower the needles.

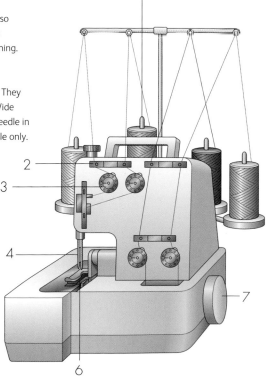

Machine feet and attachments

Most sewing machines will be supplied with a small selection of feet to aid particular sewing tasks. These will normally include a standard foot, a zipper foot, and a buttonhole foot, but there are many others available. They may vary in appearance from one make to another but are designed specifically to make each task easier.

STRAIGHT STITCH FOOT

Used for: Straight stitching (especially on fine fabric)

Sewer's notes: Replace the normal (wide hole) throat plate with a (small hole) straight stitch throat plate. This, and the straight stitch foot, holds the fabric closer to the needle and prevents it from being pushed down and jamming the mechanism.

CONCEALED ZIPPER FOOT

Used for: Inserting concealed/invisible zippers

Sewer's notes: Use the standard zipper foot on the outer edge of the zipper tape to secure it first, then feed the teeth into the concealed foot. This gets right under the teeth and the zipper will be invisible in the seam.

BLIND HEM FOOT

Used for: Quick hems on drapes and garments

Sewer's notes: The trick of perfect machine blind hemming is positioning the folded fabric. On a good blind hem foot there are guides to show where to feed the folded hem into the foot. Works best on medium and thick fabrics.

NARROW HEM OR PICOT FOOT
Used for: Narrow rolled hemming
Sewer's notes: Machine a row of straight stitches close to the edge and trim up to it. Feed this edge into the rolled hem foot, which turns it and stitches the hem. Use a straight stitch or zigzag. Available in various widths.

OVERCASTING FOOT
Used for: Neatening edges and sewing serge-like seams
Sewer's notes: The "finger" on the foot allows stitches to be formed over it without pulling on the fabric edge. Cut away the excess with shears and feed the cut edge under the finger. Use with a pre-programmed overcast stitch or zigzag.

WALKING FOOT
Used for: Long seams, hems on stretch fabric, multiple fabric layers, patchwork
Sewer's notes: This is one of the most useful feet available. The foot walks over the cloth and prevents seams from shifting along its length or stretching. Use when accuracy is essential for matching large patterns or patchwork pieces.

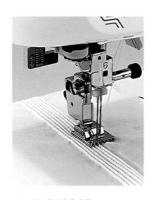

PIN TUCK FOOT
Used for: Creating twin-needle tucks to decorate fabric
Sewer's notes: A row of twin-needle tucks can be fed under the grooves of the foot, allowing further tucks to be made close and parallel to the first.

GATHERING FOOT
Used for: For ruffles and frills
Sewer's notes: Set the machine to a long straight stitch and place the fabric to be gathered uppermost. Feed the other layer in through the guide in the foot with right side down. The lower layer will be gathered and stitched to the upper layer.

CLEAR FOOT
Used for: Appliqué, embroidery, and where it is helpful to view the stitching
Sewer's notes: The clear foot often has a wide groove on the underside to help it glide over decorative stitching.

10

tips and hints

Following a few simple steps will help you get the most from your sewing machine/serger.

1

Setting up

Place the machine in a well-lit area on a large surface to give plenty of room to work. Make sure the seating is of a suitable type and height for you to sew comfortably.

2

Machine maintenance

Keep the sewing machine or serger lint- and dust-free. A build-up of lint can jam the mechanism or get caught beneath the stitches.

6

Trial stitching

Always make a trial first to eliminate problems and find the best stitch length and width before handling a project. Different fabrics sew in different ways and adjustments may be necessary.

7

Bobbins

Wind bobbins carefully and steadily. Bobbins wound too fast can cause puckered seams and if wound unevenly stitch tension may be poor or threads may break.

3

Needles

Replace needles frequently and use the type designed for the task. This will eliminate skipped stitches and damage to fabric threads.

4

Thread

Always use good quality thread. It should be evenly spun with long fibers to travel easily through the guides and produce a minimum of lint.

5

Feet and attachments

Make use of specialist presser feet. They will make the task easier and quicker as well as produce a better finished result.

8

Secure thread ends

Fasten off thread ends by a) threading them on to a needle and securing them, b) using a product to fuse or glue them, or c) tie them in a knot. This will ensure that seams won't come apart.

9

Leave a tail of threads to start

If the sewing machine does not automatically cut the threads, always leave a tail behind the needle. Otherwise, as the needle is raised to start sewing again the thread may come out of the eye.

10

Speed

Sew at a steady speed to produce even stitching. This is especially important for decorative work as stitches will not be formed accurately if the speed is too fast or erratic.

Threads

There are many types of thread available for sewing. The choice of thread will depend on whether it is for embroidery or hand stitching, or if a sewing machine or serger is being used. Choose good quality thread in a fiber similar to the fabric being used, for example cotton thread for cotton and linen fabric; polyester for synthetic cloth; silk for silk and wool fabric. Choose colors that closely match the fabric to blend in to a garment, or ones which contrast and stand out for bright, decorative finishes.

1 GENERAL-PURPOSE THREADS

These may be spun from polyester or mercerized cotton or have a cotton core covered with polyester. They are suitable for using on the sewing machine for making garments, drapes, and other "home-dec" projects. They are also available in large cones, which makes them suitable for serger sewing.

2 SILK THREAD

Reels of silk thread are ideal for sewing silk fabric and wool fabric as it comes from an animal source. However, as silk thread is expensive, polyester is often used instead. Use 100 percent silk thread for hand stitching as it is easy to handle and does not tend to knot.

3 MACHINE EMBROIDERY FLOSS

This is made from polyester or rayon as it has a high sheen to reflect the light. It is also available in cotton and even wool, and these give a matte finish with different textures.

4 METALLIC THREAD

This can be used for hand sewing and also machining. For machine embroidery a special needle with a large eye is required to prevent the thread from breaking or shredding. It is also necessary to sew at a slow steady pace with these threads.

5 WOOLY NYLON

Wooly nylon is a soft, strong, thick thread that is used in the loopers of a serger. It is ideal for flatlocking and hemming as the loosely spun thread gives better coverage of the seam or edge. It is too thick to be used in the needles of a serger.

6 HAND EMBROIDERY FLOSS

These include twisted pearl cotton, loosely wound stranded threads which can be split and used as needed, soft embroidery floss, and tapestry wools. These threads are too thick to go through machine needles but can be used in the loopers of sergers for decorative flatlocking and rolled hemming. They can also be wound on the bobbin of a sewing machine and fabric can be sewn upside down, giving bolder stitching with the thicker thread.

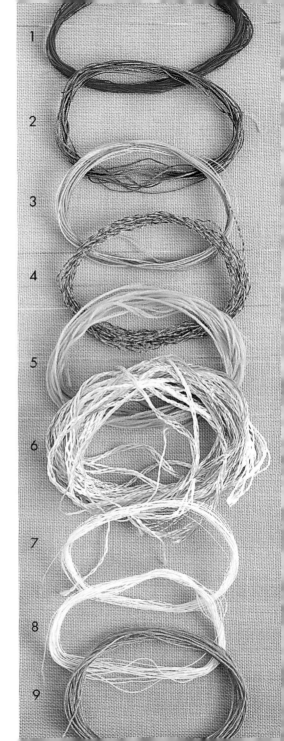

7 BOBBIN FILL

This is a fine thread normally available in black or white used in the bobbin of a sewing machine for machine embroidery. It reduces the bulk in an embroidered design and produces better embroidery stitching. It can also be bought in pre-wound bobbins to save time when stitching.

8 BASTING THREAD

This soft cotton thread is weaker than a general-purpose thread. It is therefore ideal for temporary hand sewing as it will break and not damage fabric when removed.

9 TOP STITCH THREAD

This is a stronger, thicker thread that gives a bolder finish. Use it for top stitching seams, hand sewing buttonholes, and for sewing on buttons. It should be used with a top stitch needle as it has a larger eye to carry the thread and with general-purpose thread wound on to the bobbin.

Stitch Directory

This section features both functional and decorative stitches that you can apply by hand, machine, or serger. Follow the stitch-specific advice and the step-by-step diagrams and instructions to achieve stunning results.

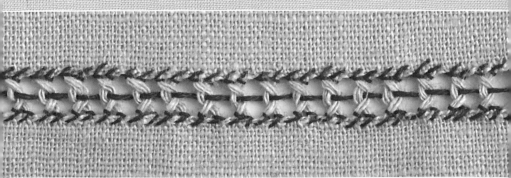

Hand stitches

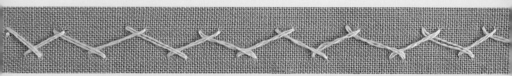

This chapter details functional hand stitches, which are ideal for making seams, hems, and finishing edges on clothes and projects for the home. Use the diagrams and step-by-step instructions to guide you through creating the stitches. The additional information offers further help, and machine alternatives are suggested when appropriate.

Double stitch

Use a double stitch at the start and end of sewing to secure the threads.

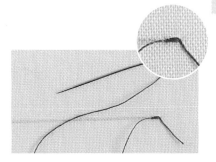

1 *Take a small stitch at the beginning of the work, going down through the fabric and back up a short distance along the sewing line, leaving a tail approximately ½ in (1.2cm) long.*

2 *Make a second stitch over the first, without pulling the thread tail through.*

3 *Repeat step 2, creating two stitches on top of each other. Pull the thread to check it is secure. If not, repeat with a third stitch.*

4 *To complete a row of stitching use two stitches on top of each other to secure the end. Snip thread tails with scissors.*

GARMENT/PROJECT

Use a double stitch to start and finish any hand sewing. For decorative work make the double stitch on the wrong side of the fabric so it will not show on the surface.

FABRIC

It may be necessary to use more than two stitches on some fabrics, especially loosely woven fabric.

NOTIONS AND STITCH SIZE

Use a cotton or cotton/polyester thread with an appropriate needle for sewing garments. Use embroidery floss and an embroidery needle for decorative work.

ALTERNATIVE

When hand sewing, a knot at the end of the thread can be used instead of a double stitch. When using a sewing machine use the reverse button to go over stitches to secure the start and finish of work.

PRESSING AND FINISHING

No special care is needed.

Running stitch

Running stitch is a simple row of stitches creating a regular dotted line of threads. Small stitches create a seam. Longer stitches are more temporary basting stitches (see page 46).

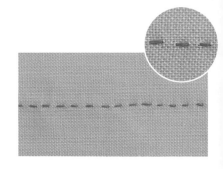

1 *Having secured the thread on the wrong side, bring the needle through to the surface at the start of the first stitch.*

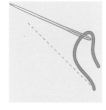

2 *Move a stitch length forward along the sewing line, take the needle down through the fabric, then bring it back up one stitch further on. The stitch and the gap will be the same size.*

3 *Continue to the end of the line.*

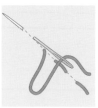

GARMENT/PROJECT

Smaller running stitches are good for seams not subject to strain. Use running stitches for easing and gathering (see page 38). Use longer running stitches (basting) for temporary sewing (see page 46).

FABRIC

Use on all fabric weights.

NOTIONS AND STITCH SIZE

Choose the needle and thread according to fabric weight. Use smaller stitches for a stronger finish and larger stitches for temporary sewing. Use embroidery floss and an embroidery needle for a decorative finish.

ALTERNATIVE

If using a sewing machine use a straight stitch (see page 52).

PRESSING AND FINISHING

No special care is needed.

Back stitch

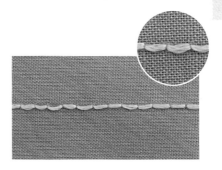

If there is no sewing machine available and there is a garment to be sewn together, this is the best hand stitch to use. It requires regular stitches for a neat result.

1 Having secured the thread on the wrong side, bring it through to the surface at the end position of the stitch.

2 Move a stitch length backward along the line, take the needle down through the fabric, and bring it back up to the surface at the end position of this stitch.

3 Move back along the line and take the needle down the same hole as the previous thread; bring it up to the surface at the end position of this stitch. Continue to the end of the line.

GARMENT/PROJECT

Back stitch is useful for any garment or sewing project where a hand seam is required. Also use it as a decorative stitch.

FABRIC

Use on any fabric. It's especially useful for those with a small amount of stretch.

NOTIONS AND STITCH SIZE

Use a fine needle with cotton or polyester thread. Use an embroidery needle and suitable thread when using back stitch for decorative work.

ALTERNATIVE

If using a sewing machine, use a straight stitch (see page 52), or use a reinforcement stitch/stretch stitch (see page 55) if some "give" is required.

PRESSING AND FINISHING

No special care is needed.

Tailor's tacks

Tailor's tacks are loose basting stitches. They mark the position of paper pattern symbols and remain in the fabric when the pattern is taken off. They are removed when no longer needed.

Reverse

Front

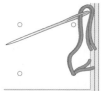

1 *Use a double thread in a contrasting color to the fabric. Take the needle down through the paper of the pattern symbol and through the two layers of fabric below. Bring the needle back up, leaving the original tail approximately 2 in. (5cm) long on the surface.*

2 *Take the needle down through the fabric again, leaving a loop of thread on the surface. Bring the needle back to the surface and cut the thread, leaving a tail of approximately 2 in. (5cm).*

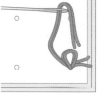

3 *Remove the paper pattern carefully. Ease the two layers of fabric apart and snip the threads between, leaving threads on both pieces of fabric.*

GARMENT/PROJECT

Tailor's tacks are useful for marking the positions of pockets, darts, buttonholes, and buttons.

FABRIC

Use on all types of fabric, but take care on looser weaves as the threads from the tacks may fall out.

NOTIONS AND STITCH SIZE

Use a contrasting color of basting thread in double thickness. Use small, loose stitches.

ALTERNATIVE

There is no machine alternative to tailor's tacks. Tailor's tacks are an accurate means of transferring pattern markings, best done by hand.

PRESSING AND FINISHING

When handling and ironing the fabric, take care not to lose the threads from the tailor's tacks before they are required.

Blanket stitch

Traditionally used to edge blankets, blanket stitch is now more of a decorative stitch worked in embroidery floss.

1 *Secure the thread, and bring the needle through on the edge of the fabric.*

2 *Bring the needle through from the back of the fabric to the surface, on the stitching line. Loop the single end of the thread under the needle, then pull the needle through carefully. Adjust the stitch so that it lies on the edge of the fabric.*

3 *Repeat to create evenly spaced stitches along the edge of the fabric. Pull the threads gently to avoid distorting the stitches or the fabric.*

GARMENT/PROJECT

Blanket stitch is suitable for blankets, tablecloths, and bedding as a functional and decorative edge. It is also used on jacket edgings in a contrasting thread to create a decorative finish.

FABRIC

This is a good stitch for medium to heavyweight fabrics, such as wool or fleece. Use it on lightweight cottons and linens to create an heirloom or vintage effect.

NOTIONS AND STITCH SIZE

Use an embroidery needle to suit the weight of cloth with a large enough eye to take the embroidery floss being used.

ALTERNATIVE

A machine blanket stitch is available on some sewing machines. Use it with a wing needle (see page 143) to achieve an heirloom effect.

PRESSING AND FINISHING

When used as a decorative stitch, take care not to flatten the threads with the iron. Use a soft, thick pad below the stitches and protect the surface with a soft, thick pressing cloth.

Buttonhole stitch

Buttonhole stitch is very similar to blanket stitch but the stitches are worked close together. It makes a stronger finished edge.

1 *Secure the thread and bring the needle through on the edge of the fabric. Bring the needle through from the back of the fabric to the surface, on the stitching line. Loop the single end of the thread under the needle, then pull the needle through carefully. Adjust the stitch so that it lies on the edge of the fabric.*

2 *Bring the needle through from the back of the fabric to the surface, next to the first stitch without leaving a gap. Loop the single end of the thread under the needle, then pull through carefully.*

3 *Repeat to create a row of stitches along the edge of the fabric.*

GARMENT/PROJECT

Use buttonhole stitch to produce buttonholes or to form a strong, neat finish to an edge. It is also a decorative stitch for embroidery.

FABRIC

Use on fine, lightweight, natural fabrics to create an heirloom or vintage effect. Buttonhole stitch also works well on heavier and thicker fabric to prevent fraying.

NOTIONS AND STITCH SIZE

Select needle and stitch size according to the weight of the cloth. Use a large eye needle to take embroidery floss.

ALTERNATIVE

Modern sewing machines offer a choice of buttonholes that are easy to make. To neaten an edge use a close zigzag stitch and sew ⅝ in. (1.5cm) in from the edge, then trim away the excess fabric.

PRESSING AND FINISHING

For embroidery or decorative buttonhole stitches press lightly from the wrong side so as not to flatten the threads.

Hemming

Hemming is a row of small, slanting stitches, which hold a hem in place. It is a secure way of finishing a hem.

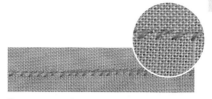

Reverse

Front

1 *Fold up the hem and secure the end of the thread in the hem fold with a double stitch.*

2 *Using a small, slanting stitch pick up one or two threads from the fabric. Next catch the fold of the hem with the needle and pull the thread through.*

3 *Repeat along the fold of the hem, creating a row of small, regular stitches.*

GARMENT/PROJECT

Use hemming to finish skirts, pants, and sleeves.

FABRIC

Use on thicker fabrics where the stitches disappear in the depth of the cloth. The stitches will be visible from the right side of a fine, thin fabric. Use it to finish the inside of a waistband on pants or skirts.

NOTIONS AND STITCH SIZE

Use a fine needle that will not leave holes in the fabric. Use thread that is a good color match, or one shade darker as it will be less visible if it shows through to the surface of the fabric.

ALTERNATIVE

Slip stitch and lock stitch are good alternative hand-hemming methods. Use a blind hemming stitch, in conjunction with a blind hem foot, on the sewing machine.

PRESSING AND FINISHING

Press lightly from the wrong side on a well-padded ironing board to prevent a ridge showing along the hem.

Slip stitch

Slip stitch is a hemming stitch which is almost invisible on both the right and wrong sides.

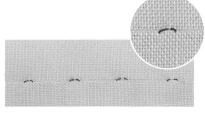

Reverse

Front

1 *Secure the end of the thread in the fold with a double stitch.*

2 *Pick up one or two threads of the fabric with the needle, then slip the needle through the fold of the hem. Bring the needle out ¼ in. (0.6cm) away and pick up another couple of stitches before returning through the fold of the hem.*

3 *As the row of stitches progresses, pull lightly to tighten the thread, but not too much to avoid distorting the fabric and making the stitches more obvious.*

GARMENT/PROJECT

Use slip stitch to hem a garment in a lightweight fabric where hemming stitch isn't suitable. Use it to attach linings or trimmings.

FABRIC

Use slip stitch when hemming lightweight fabrics.

NOTIONS AND STITCH SIZE

Use a small needle and small hand stitches to get a secure finish.

ALTERNATIVE

Use hemming, lock stitch, or herringbone stitch as alternative hand-hem finishes, or a blind hemming stitch in conjunction with a blind hem foot if using a sewing machine.

PRESSING AND FINISHING

Press lightly from the wrong side on a well-padded ironing board to prevent a ridge showing along the hem.

Ladder stitch

Like slip stitch, this is almost invisible. Use ladder stitch to sew a small area of a seam from the right side or to join two edges together to close an opening, for example when finishing a cushion cover or soft toy.

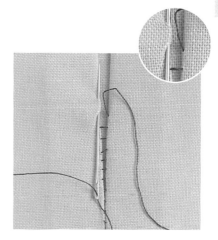

1 *Secure the end of the thread in one of the folded edges with a double stitch.*

2 *Take a small stitch on the fold opposite, taking the needle ⅛ in. (0.3cm) through the fold. Cross back to the first folded edge and repeat. This creates a ladder-like stitch between the edges, and when the thread is pulled they close together, hiding the stitches.*

3 *Continue and complete the seam, securing the thread ends.*

GARMENT/PROJECT

Use ladder stitch on small seams and openings which cannot be sewn from behind, such as in soft toys and cushions. Use it to attach trimmings.

FABRIC

Use on all weights of fabric.

NOTIONS AND STITCH SIZE

Use a small needle and small stitches to make a strong finish.

ALTERNATIVE

There is no sewing machine alternative; ladder stitch is used when a seam cannot be sewn from behind and has to be finished from the front of the work by hand.

PRESSING AND FINISHING

Use the iron to flatten the ladder stitches when sewing is completed.

Lock stitch

Use this hemming stitch for clothes and drapes. The benefit of a lock stitch hem is its ability to hold together when the thread breaks. As each stitch is independent the hem will not unravel fully. Only a small area will need to be repaired rather than the entire hem.

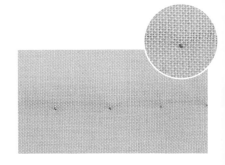

1 *Secure the thread with a double stitch in the hem.*

2 *Pick up one or two threads of the fabric on the stitching line and some threads on the hem adjacent to this.*

3 *Pull the thread until almost through, then take the needle through the loop created by the thread. Pull gently to complete the stitch.*

4 *Repeat the stitches, making them about ½–¾ in. (1.2–1.8cm) apart. The further apart they are the less obvious they will be from the right side.*

GARMENT/PROJECT

Use lock stitch for all garment and drape hems which require an invisible finish.

FABRIC

Lock stitch works well on all fabrics, but is especially useful on those with a stretch.

NOTIONS AND STITCH SIZE

Use a fine needle that will not leave holes in the fabric. Keep stitches long and regular so that they will not be seen from the right side.

ALTERNATIVE

Like lock stitch, a herringbone stitch will allow a fabric to stretch. Some sewing machines have a blind hem stitch suitable for stretch fabrics.

PRESSING AND FINISHING

As with all hems, press lightly from behind to prevent a ridge becoming visible along the hem.

Overcasting

Overcasting is a hand stitch used to neaten a raw edge to prevent it from fraying. It is also used to join two pieces of non-fraying fabric.

Joining fabric together

Neatening an edge

1 *Working close to the edge of the fabric, bring the needle through from the back to the surface of the work.*

2 *Take the needle over the raw edge and back through to the surface again.*

3 *Continue in this way, making a row of diagonal stitches over the raw edge of the fabric to neaten it. Do not pull the stitches too tightly as this will curl the edge of the cloth.*

Sewer's tip

Use closer stitches if the fabric frays badly.

GARMENT/PROJECT

Use overcasting on any fabric edge which might fray when a hand-sewn finish is required. Also use it to join fabrics which do not fray. Overcasting is used to join patchwork pieces.

FABRIC

Use on all fabrics to neaten raw edges which fray. If the fabric frays badly, sew the stitches closer together. Use also on non-fraying fabric to join pieces together, similar to flatlocking on a serger (see pages 67–68).

NOTIONS AND STITCH SIZE

Use a fine needle and good quality cotton or polyester sewing thread.

ALTERNATIVE

Use a zigzag stitch (see page 53) or specialist overcasting stitch (see page 57) on a sewing machine, or finish raw edges with a serger (see pages 64–68). Machine methods are much quicker and used more often today.

PRESSING AND FINISHING

Press the edges flat when stitching is completed.

Gathering and easing

Gathering is created by hand using a row of running stitches to control fullness of cloth. The smaller the stitches, the smaller the gathers. Easing refers to a small amount of fabric being pulled up without any visible tucks or gathers.

1 *Secure the thread tightly on the sewing line and sew up and down through the fabric to create a row of even running stitches.*

2 *Pull the thread up to reduce the fabric to the desired length.*

3 *Secure the thread end by wrapping it around a pin and distribute the gathers evenly along the length. Sew as required.*

GARMENT/PROJECT

Gathering and easing is useful for skirt waists before they are attached to a waistband, and for sleeve heads and cuffs.

FABRIC

Although most fabrics can be gathered, lightweight and fine fabrics show gathers off well.

NOTIONS AND STITCH SIZE

Use a fine needle of medium to long length to make gathers quickly, as three or four stitches can be sewn at one time. Use a double length of thread for extra strength.

ALTERNATIVE

Gathering is more often done on a sewing machine. Use the longest straight stitch available. For rows of gathers see gauging (page 44).

PRESSING AND FINISHING

Gathers will be flattened by ironing.

Prick stitch

Prick stitch is similar to back stitch, where only a tiny stitch is visible on the surface of the fabric with a longer stitch on the underside. It is used for putting in zippers by hand and also for finishing an edge on a tailored jacket or coat.

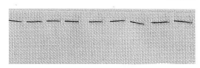

Front

Reverse

1 *Having secured the thread on the wrong side bring the needle through to the surface at the end of the first stitch.*

2 *Take a tiny stitch backward along the sewing line, then take the needle down through the fabric and bring it back up one stitch further on.*

3 *Make another tiny stitch backward and continue, creating a line of small dots on the surface with a space between. The space should be larger than the stitch, but the stitches evenly placed.*

GARMENT/PROJECT

In couture sewing prick stitch is used to put in zippers. Prick stitch is also used along the edge of a collar on a jacket or coat for a tailored finish.

FABRIC

Used on dress-weight fabric for zipper insertion and on woolen cloth for jacket and coat collars.

NOTIONS AND STITCH SIZE

A short, fine needle is useful for sewing prick stitch. Use any thread suitable for the fabric being used, but silk thread is ideal as it slides through the material easily and works well in couture sewing and tailoring. Make stitches ¼ in. (0.6cm) apart or more.

ALTERNATIVE

Use a normal length straight stitch if using a sewing machine.

PRESSING AND FINISHING

No specific care is required.

Herringbone stitch

Herringbone stitch is used for holding two layers of fabric together. Its construction makes it ideal for stretch fabrics as the stitches move with the cloth.

Front

Reverse

1 *Working from the left and on two parallel sewing lines, bring the needle to the surface on the lower sewing line.*

2 *Move a stitch length to the right and make a small horizontal stitch on the upper sewing line. Keep the thread below the needle.*

3 *Move a stitch length to the right and make a small horizontal stitch on the lower sewing line. Keep the thread above the needle.*

4 *Continue forming these two stitches to complete the work.*

GARMENT/PROJECT

Use herringbone stitch to join two layers of fabric. Use it to take up hems on stretch fabric and for tailoring when attaching tapes. It is also an embroidery stitch.

FABRIC

Use on all types of fabric, but especially stretch fabrics.

NOTIONS AND STITCH SIZE

Use a short or medium length needle for functional stitching and tailoring. Use a large eye embroidery needle for decorative work.

ALTERNATIVE

It is not possible to recreate a herringbone stitch on a sewing machine, although some machines may offer a decorative stitch that resembles it in appearance.

PRESSING AND FINISHING

Do not iron over a decorative herringbone stitch if worked in embroidery floss as this will flatten the stitches. For a hem, press lightly from the wrong side on a well-padded ironing board to prevent a ridge showing.

Bar tacks

A bar tack is a decorative reinforcement used on areas of stress, such as pockets and buttonholes.

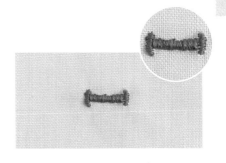

1 *Take three or four long stitches through all layers of fabric in the position required.*

2 *Starting at one end, sew around these long stitches catching some fabric threads beneath, working to the opposite end. Keep stitches close together to create a strong bar.*

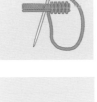

3 *In the same way, make smaller bars across each end of the bar tack to finish.*

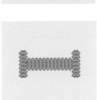

GARMENT/PROJECT

Use bar tacks on buttonholes and across the ends of pockets for extra strength.

FABRIC

Use on all weights of fabric where added strength is required.

NOTIONS AND STITCH SIZE

A medium length needle with buttonhole thread or embroidery floss is best. Keep stitches neat and regular as they are visible on a garment.

ALTERNATIVE

Sewing machines often include a bar tack stitch. This is produced using closely placed zigzag stitches and provides the same function as a hand-worked bar tack.

PRESSING AND FINISHING

No special care is required.

Sewer's tip

A blanket stitch (see page 31) can be used if preferred.

French tacks

A French tack is a bar which joins two pieces of fabric together loosely. It is used to hold lining and coat fabric together at the hem.

1 *Hold the two parts which are to be sewn together slightly apart. Secure the thread in one side and sew a small stitch in the opposite side. Repeat between the two parts three or four times.*

2 *Working from one side, wrap the threads with buttonhole stitch until the whole bar is covered. Keep the stitches close together.*

GARMENT/PROJECT

French tacks are most often used to hold a lining close to the hem of a coat without restricting it.

FABRIC

Use on all weights of fabric.

NOTIONS AND STITCH SIZE

Use a short or medium length fine needle. Make finished tacks approximately ½ in. (1.2cm) long.

ALTERNATIVE

A sewing machine cannot recreate a French tack. An alternative hand-sewing method is to use a chain to connect the two areas of fabric. Secure the thread on one section and create a chain stitch (see page 104) until the desired length is achieved, then secure to the other fabric section.

PRESSING AND FINISHING

A French tack does not require ironing.

Whipping

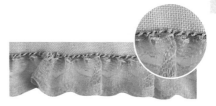

Like overcasting, whipping is a diagonal stitch sewn over the edge of cloth. Use it for finishing or gathering an edge.

Front

Reverse

1 *Working close to the edge of the fabric or lace, bring the needle through from the back to the surface of the work.*

2 *Take the needle over the raw edge and back through to the surface again.*

3 *Continue in this way, making a row of diagonal stitches over the raw edge of the fabric.*

4 *If required for gathering, pull the thread to create gathers on the edge then sew as required.*

GARMENT/PROJECT

Use to neaten raw edges, or to gather lace before stitching in place.

FABRIC

Use on all fabrics to neaten raw edges which fray. If the fabric frays badly, sew the stitches closer together.

NOTIONS AND STITCH SIZE

Use a short or medium length fine needle. Keep stitches close together and regular.

ALTERNATIVE

To neaten a raw edge use a zigzag stitch (see page 53) or specialist overcasting stitch (see page 57) on a sewing machine, or finish raw edges with a serger (see pages 64–68). A sewing machine does not recreate a whipped edge for gathering though.

PRESSING AND FINISHING

Press the edges flat when stitching is completed, being careful not to flatten any gathers when the edge has been pulled up.

Gauging

Gauging is a means of gathering by hand. Two or more rows of gathers are used to gather and control fullness in fabric. It is used to prepare fabric before it is attached to a second piece being smocked.

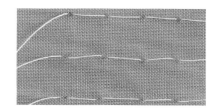

1 *Secure the thread end in the fabric, and working on the right side make a long stitch on the sewing line, taking the needle down through the fabric.*

2 *Bring the needle back up to the surface, making a shorter stitch on the wrong side. Complete the row with regular long stitches on the surface and shorter ones on the wrong side.*

3 *Make a second row (and subsequent rows) parallel to the first, ensuring the stitches are all in line.*

GARMENT/PROJECT

Use gauging to prepare fabric for smocking or for attaching cuffs and waistbands. Frills on skirts or cushions can also be made this way.

FABRIC

Light- and mediumweight fabrics like cotton lawn or shirting. Not suitable for very heavy fabrics.

NOTIONS AND STITCH SIZE

A long needle will make gauging easier, with strong, good quality thread which will not break when pulling up. Stitches should be long on top and shorter on the underside of the fabric.

ALTERNATIVES

A machine stitch will create stitches of an even length and will not give short and long stitches as required. A pleater is a gadget specifically designed to gauge fabric in readiness for smocking or making frills.

PRESSING AND FINISHING

Do not iron once the threads have been pulled to create the gathers as this will flatten them. Iron in to the tucks from the wide part of the fabric.

Darning

Darning was traditionally a means of mending tears and holes in garments, but is not used as often today.

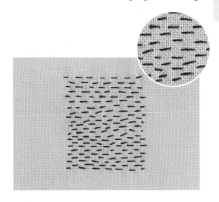

1 *Using matching colored thread, preferably a weak thread and not highly spun, pull the tear or hole together as well as possible then cover the damaged area with stitches as follows.*

2 *Work from the top right to top left making a regular running stitch across the top edge of the area to be darned.*

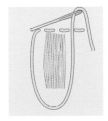

3 *Turn the work and continue to work from right to left, sewing a second row of regular running stitch above the first. The stitches should lie in between those in the row below and not directly under them.*

4 *Continue to turn and create rows of running stitches until the weakened area is covered.*

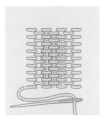

GARMENT/PROJECT

Darning was traditionally used to mend clothing, bedding, and tablewear. Darning stitch is also a decorative stitch often carried out on evenweave fabric.

FABRIC

Use on all types and weights of fabric.

NOTIONS AND STITCH SIZE

Use matching colored thread of a similar or lighter weight and a long needle. Stitches should be kept small and even.

ALTERNATIVES

Darning can be carried out with a sewing machine using rows of straight stitch or a three-step zigzag.

PRESSING AND FINISHING

Iron the darned area when completed.

Basting

Basting is a row of long, loose, temporary stitches used to hold pieces of fabric together before sewing.

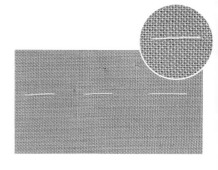

1 *Having secured the thread lightly on the wrong side, bring the needle through to the surface at the start of the first stitch.*

2 *Move a stitch length forward along the sewing line, take the needle down through the fabric, then bring it back up one stitch further on. The stitch and the gap will be the same size.*

3 *Continue to the end of the line.*

GARMENT/PROJECT

Basting is used whenever temporary stitching is required. It holds pieces of a garment together to make machining easier. Basting stitches are removed later when they are not required.

FABRIC

Use on all weights of fabric.

NOTIONS AND STITCH SIZE

Use a medium length needle and thread in a contrasting color. Basting thread does not need to be strong as it must not damage the fabric when it is removed. Basting stitches are longer than running stitches, although the technique is the same.

ALTERNATIVE

Use the longest stitch length when using a sewing machine for basting.

PRESSING AND FINISHING

Do not iron basting stitches.

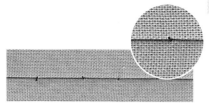

Slip basting

Slip basting is temporary stitching which holds two pieces of fabric together when plaid, striped, or patterned cloth has to be matched.

Front

Reverse

1 *Fold back the seam allowance on one side and place it over the other.*

2 *Secure the thread in the fold and take a small stitch into the seam line beside it.*

3 *Bring the needle up a stitch length further on then back through the fold on the other side.*

4 *Continue taking small stitches to join the pieces. Tiny stitches will be seen from the front and a row of basting on the seam line on the wrong side.*

GARMENT/PROJECT

Use slip basting when it is important to match plaids or patterned fabric, for example seams on pants, skirts, and dresses, and also when joining drape lengths.

FABRIC

Use on all weights of fabric with dominant prints, stripes, or plaids.

NOTIONS AND STITCH SIZE

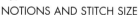

Use a fine, short needle and keep stitches ¼ in. (0.6cm) to ½ in. (1.2cm) long to hold the fabrics together securely for machining.

ALTERNATIVE

A sewing machine does not offer a suitable alternative when two pieces of patterned cloth need to be joined accurately.

PRESSING AND FINISHING

Press the upper section of fabric along the seam line initially to help with matching the pattern. When finished, press the seam open.

Diagonal basting

Diagonal basting is used to attach layers of fabric together before machining. It is a temporary stitch and is used to hold interfacing, interlining, or lining to the wrong side of a fabric.

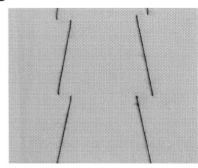

1 *Make a horizontal stitch through both or all layers, taking the needle down on the right and back up to the surface on the left.*

2 *Make the second stitch below and parallel to the first, creating a diagonal stitch which slants from top left to bottom right. Continue the row in this way.*

3 *Make a second row of stitching, mirroring the first, then continue making rows until the two pieces are sewn together.*

GARMENT/PROJECT

Use diagonal basting to attach interfacing to jacket pieces before construction, and interlining to skirt panels to avoid seating. It can also be used to control pleats.

FABRIC

Diagonal basting is normally used to join two different fabrics together.

NOTIONS AND STITCH SIZE

Use a small needle and basting thread. Make the stitches long and do not pull them too tight.

ALTERNATIVE

Hand diagonal basting is the best method for attaching layers, but a long straight machine stitch may be useful in some circumstances. Alternatively, use a fusible interfacing if appropriate.

PRESSING AND FINISHING

Do not iron the layers while the basting is in place as this may leave the fabric with thread lines.

Pad stitching

Similar to diagonal basting, pad stitching is used in tailoring to attach interfacings to collars and lapels. It is a permanent stitch and is not visible from the right side.

1
Make a tiny horizontal stitch through the interfacing, catching a thread or two of the main fabric below. Take the needle down on the right and back up to the surface on the left.

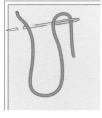

2
Make the second stitch below and parallel to the first, creating a diagonal stitch which slants from top left to bottom right. Continue the row in this way.

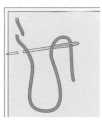

3
Make a second row of stitching, mirroring the first, then continue making rows until the two pieces are sewn together.

GARMENT/PROJECT
Use pad stitching on tailored garments to attach interfacing to the collar and lapels.

FABRIC
Use on tailoring canvases and all weights of suiting.

NOTIONS AND STITCH SIZE
Use a small, fine needle with silk thread for best results and make small, secure stitches.

ALTERNATIVE
There are no sewing machine alternatives, but fusible interfacing is available which does away with hand stitching.

PRESSING AND FINISHING
Use steam to shape the collar and lapel when the pad stitching is in place.

Sewing machine stitches

The stitches in this chapter are available on all modern machines. They are basic and functional, enabling seaming, finishing, and more decorative tasks to be carried out. The diagrams and instructions will help you set the machine correctly and sew the stitch required. Follow the additional advice to ensure the best possible finish.

Securing threads

It is important to secure the threads at the start and finish of a seam so that the stitching does not unravel. This is easy to do using the reverse button on a sewing machine as it traps the stitches, making them less likely to work free.

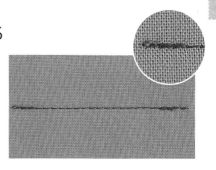

1 *At the start of a row of stitching, lower the needle into the fabric then lower the presser foot. Machine three stitches forward then stop.*

2 *Sew back over these stitches and stop*

3 *Continue forward again over these stitches and complete the row.*

4 *Reverse over the last three stitches then continue once again to the end. Raise the presser foot and needle and cut thread tails. The threads will now be secure.*

GARMENT/PROJECT

Use reverse stitching to secure threads on all seams when using a sewing machine.

FABRIC

Use on all types and weights of fabric.

NOTIONS AND STITCH SIZE

Use a needle and stitch suitable for the fabric and project.

ALTERNATIVE

An alternative to reversing over stitches is to thread the loose "tails" onto a needle and sew the ends into the seam to secure them.

PRESSING AND FINISHING

No specific instructions are necessary.

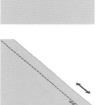

Straight stitch

A straight stitch is the original and most useful machine stitch available. It is very versatile and will allow most techniques to be undertaken, for example seams, darts, tucks, and gathering.

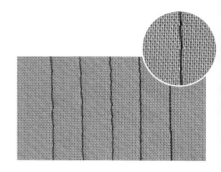

1 *Check the sewing machine manual and set for straight stitch.*

2 *Sew the seam in the position required, securing both ends (see page 51).*

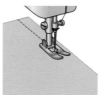

GARMENT/PROJECT

Use this versatile stitch for everything from seaming to attaching lace, basting to gathering.

FABRIC

Use on all types and weights of fabric, adjusting the stitch length if necessary.

NOTIONS AND STITCH SIZE

Use needles according to the type of fabric chosen (see pages 14–15). For fine fabric use a short stitch of 16 stitches to 1 in. (2mm); for mediumweight fabric use 12 stitches to 1 in. (2.5mm); for heavy or thick fabric use a long stitch of 8 to 10 stitches to 1 in. (3mm).

ALTERNATIVE

Use a running stitch or a back stitch if sewing by hand.

PRESSING AND FINISHING

No specific care is required.

Zigzag stitch

A zigzag stitch is very versatile as the length and width of the stitches can be adjusted to suit different projects such as sewing stretch fabrics, neatening raw edges, and attaching elastic.

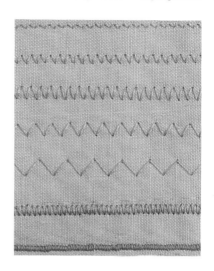

1 *Set the machine for zigzag and adjust the length and width to suit the task. Use the manual as a guide and test the stitch on spare fabric first.*

2 *Place the needle into the fabric at the start of the sewing line. Lower the presser foot and sew.*

GARMENT/PROJECT

Use a wide zigzag for finishing edges or attaching elastic and a narrow zigzag when seaming stretch fabric.

FABRIC

Use on all fabric types and weights, varying length and width as necessary.

NOTIONS AND STITCH SIZE

Choose a needle to suit the fabric weight. Use a stretch or ball point needle for sewing stretch fabric. The size of the zigzag stitch will depend on the task.

ALTERNATIVE

For neatening an edge, use an overcast stitch worked by hand, or if sewing a seam in a stretch fabric, use a hand-sewn back stitch.

PRESSING AND FINISHING

No special instructions.

Three-step zigzag stitch

A three-point or three-step zigzag is used for neatening edges for medium- to heavyweight and stretch fabric. It is also a good stitch to use to attach elastic. Its three-step nature makes it useful when a wider stitch is required as it does not tend to pull up fabric as a very wide traditional zigzag might do.

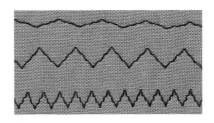

1 *Carry out a trial first to get the stitch length and width suitable for the task.*

2 *When sewing on an edge, allow the needle to drop off the fabric when in the far right position.*

Sewer's tip

When attaching elastic the stitches will appear closer when finished as the fabric is stretched during stitching.

GARMENT/PROJECT

Use three-point zigzag for attaching elastic to the edge of fabric, for example when sewing lingerie or swimwear. It can also be used to finish and neaten raw edges on medium- to heavyweight fabric, or to attach ribbon or lace for decoration.

FABRIC

Use on all types of material; it is most useful for stretch fabrics and medium- to heavyweight cloth.

NOTIONS AND STITCH SIZE

Use a ball point or stretch needle when sewing this stitch on stretchy fabric. For fine fabric use a size 9 or 11 needle; for mediumweight fabric use a size 11 or 14 needle; for thick or heavy material use a size 16 or 18 needle. Check stitch length and width on a sample first.

ALTERNATIVE

Use a hand-worked overcasting stitch to neaten raw edges. To attach elastic by hand, make a casing and thread the elastic through it.

PRESSING AND FINISHING

When used to neaten an edge, press with an iron to flatten it. Press only lightly when used to sew elastic in place.

Stretch stitch

A stretch stitch has some "give" in it so that, as the fabric stretches, the seam moves with it and the thread does not break. It is either produced by a row of narrow zigzag stitches which straighten when pulled, or with a triple stitch that produces stitches going back and forth along the seam line.

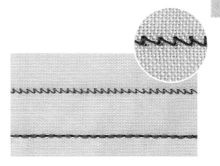

1 *Refer to the sewing machine manual for the stitch settings. If a stretch stitch is not available set it to a zigzag stitch with a narrow setting.*

2 *Position the needle at the start of the sewing line, lower the presser foot and sew.*

GARMENT/PROJECT

Use stretch stitch for all garments and projects made with stretch fabric.

FABRIC

Use on knitted and spandex fabrics of any weight. It ensures the threads will not break when the fabric stretches.

NOTIONS AND STITCH SIZE

Use ball point or stretch needles. Set stitches to zigzag: 12 to 14 stitches per 1 in. (2mm), approximately $\frac{1}{16}$–$\frac{1}{8}$ in. (1–3mm) wide.

ALTERNATIVE

Use back stitch as an alternative hand stitch, or use a serger which copes well with stretch fabrics.

PRESSING AND FINISHING

Pressing may take out any rippling in the seam, but if not use a walking foot attachment.

Sewer's tip

If the seam ripples after sewing, change the presser foot for a walking foot attachment.

Basting

Temporary seams are made by basting fabric pieces together with a long machine stitch. Basting can be used for fitting a garment before construction, or for holding the fabric together to aid final sewing.

1 *Set the sewing machine to straight stitch at the longest stitch setting.*

2 *Pin the fabric pieces together and machine on the sewing line, removing the pins in the process.*

GARMENT/PROJECT

Use basting for fitting a garment before sewing it together, or for holding seams in place for stitching.

FABRIC

Use on all fabric weights and types.

NOTIONS AND STITCH SIZE

Use a needle suitable for the task and fabric then set the stitch to the longest straight stitch.

ALTERNATIVE

A hand basting stitch (page 46) could be used.

PRESSING AND FINISHING

Do not iron basting as it is a temporary stitch and pressing may leave an impression in the fabric.

Overcasting

Although edges can be finished with a zigzag stitch, some machines provide a specific overcasting stitch to cover the raw edges. This stitch is best used with a dedicated presser foot as it prevents the edges from curling in.

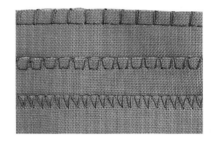

1 *Choose a suitable overcasting stitch and carry out a trial on spare fabric.*

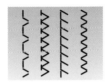

2 *Change the presser foot to an "overcasting" foot.*

3 *Place the fabric edge next to the foot guide and sew, feeding the fabric through against the guide.*

GARMENT/PROJECT

Finish all raw edges with this stitch and the overcasting foot.

FABRIC

There are different overcasting stitches for different types and weights of fabric. Choose the most suitable from the manual.

NOTIONS AND STITCH SIZE

Use the correct needle for the fabric (see page 14). Set the stitch width to fall just over the edge of the fabric. If the stitch is not wide enough the needle could break, as it may hit the bar on the presser foot.

ALTERNATIVE

Use a zigzag stitch or a serger.

PRESSING AND FINISHING

Press the edges flat once finished.

Blind hemming

A blind hemming stitch is available on some sewing machine models. By folding the fabric carefully and using a presser foot designed for blind hemming a neat, almost invisible, hem can be created.

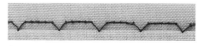

Reverse

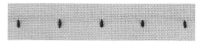

Front

1 *Fold up the hem to the finished length, then fold the body of the fabric back on itself leaving the hem flat. Pin the hem in place.*

2 *Set the sewing machine to blind hemming stitch and change the presser foot.*

3 *Place the hem under the needle and place the fold against the guide on the presser foot. Sew through the hem, catching the fold when the needle swings to the left.*

GARMENT/PROJECT

Use machine blind hemming for drapes, pants, skirts, and dresses.

FABRIC

Machine blind hemming is suitable for medium to thick fabrics as the stitches are less visible from the right side. It is not suitable for lightweight or sheer fabrics.

NOTIONS AND STITCH SIZE

Use a size 14 or 16 needle as fabric will be heavier. Space the stitches as wide as the machine will allow so that they will be further apart and less visible from the right side.

ALTERNATIVES

Use slip stitch, lock stitch, or herring bone stitch by hand.

PRESSING AND FINISHING

First press the hem carefully from the wrong side, sliding the point of the iron under the loose edge. Next, turn over and press the bottom fold of the hem, taking care not to iron over the inside edge as this will create a ridge on the right side.

Gathering

Although gathering can be carried out by hand, it is much faster when done by machine.

1 *Mark the gathering position with tailor's tacks or pins and set the sewing machine to the longest straight stitch. Before placing the fabric under the presser foot, make sure there is a tail of threads at least 3 in. (7.5cm) long. This makes pulling up the threads easier.*

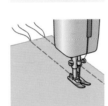

2 *Sew a row of long stitches ⅛ in. (3mm) from the sewing line in the seam allowance. Sew a second line of gathering stitches ⅛ in. (3mm) on the other side of the sewing line. Leave a tail of threads at the end of the row and do not secure the threads at either end.*

3 *Pull up the fabric to create gathers until the correct length is achieved. Wrap the threads around pins placed at the ends. Spread the gathers evenly and sew as required.*

Sewer's tip

If gathering a long length of fabric, divide the length into shorter sections, for example halves or quarters, and gather each one in turn.

GARMENT/PROJECT

Gathering is used as a design feature on ladies' and children's clothing to control fabric fullness. Use it to create frills on bedding and cushions.

FABRIC

Use on light- to mediumweight fabric for best results.

NOTIONS AND STITCH SIZE

Use a size 11 needle (unless a heavier fabric is being gathered) and set the stitch length at the longest straight stitch.

ALTERNATIVE

Use hand gathering (page 38), corded gathering (page 60), or gauging (page 44). A gathering foot attachment can be used to gather one length of fabric to another. It gathers one length as it is fed under the needle, sewing it to a length of fabric lying on top. This eliminates a stage when sewing.

PRESSING AND FINISHING

Do not press the gathers as this will flatten them. When gathers are sewn in position, iron from the fullness of the fabric into the gathered folds with the point of the iron.

Corded gathering

This is a quick method and is ideal when gathering a heavier weight fabric, for example large drapes.

1 *Set the sewing machine to the longest and largest zigzag stitch.*

2 *Cut a length of fine cord 5 in. (12.5cm) longer than the required length. Pin it at intervals just above the gathering line in the seam allowance (approximately ¼ in. [0.6cm] from the raw edge), leaving a tail of cord at either end.*

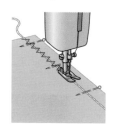

3 *Place the presser foot over the cord and zigzag along its length, taking care not to catch the cord with the stitching.*

4 *Pull up the fabric along the cord, creating gathers, and spread them evenly along the length. This gathered section can now be pinned and sewn in position on the sewing line. Pull out the cord when stitched in place.*

GARMENT/PROJECT

Use corded gathering on a garment made with heavier weight fabric. Large drapes can be gathered using this method.

FABRIC

Use for thick or heavyweight fabrics or large sections when machine sewing thread might break.

NOTIONS AND STITCH SIZE

Use a size 14 or 16 needle and the longest, widest, zigzag setting available.

ALTERNATIVE

Use hand gathering (page 38) or gathering (page 59).

PRESSING AND FINISHING

Do not press the gathers as this will flatten them. When gathers are sewn in position, iron from the fullness of the fabric into the gathered folds with the point of the iron.

Darning

Darning was traditionally a means of mending tears and holes in garments, but is not used as often today.

1 *Cut a patch of fabric and baste this to the underside of the tear or hole. Using matching colored thread set up the sewing machine with a three-step zigzag stitch.*

2 *Work with the surface of the work uppermost and from the outside edge of the area to be darned. Sew a row of three-step zigzag stitch across the area.*

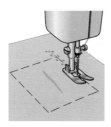

3 *At the end of the row leave the needle in the fabric, lift the presser foot, and turn the fabric 180 degrees. Machine a second row partly over the first.*

4 *Repeat steps 2 and 3 to cover and strengthen the area, then remove basting.*

GARMENTS/PROJECTS

Darning was traditionally used to mend clothing, bedding, and tableware.

FABRIC

Use on all types and weights of fabric.

NOTIONS AND STITCH SIZE

Use matching colored thread and a standard machine needle to suit the weight of the cloth (see page 14). Use a three-step zigzag, a plain zigzag, or closely placed straight stitches.

ALTERNATIVES

See darning by hand (page 45).

PRESSING AND FINISHING

Iron the darned area when completed.

Stay stitching

Stay stitching is a line of regular straight stitches sewn in the seam allowance (just inside the sewing line) used to prevent fabric, cut off grain, from stretching. The stitches hold the single layer of fabric in shape until sewn permanently.

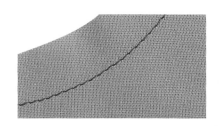

1 *Set the machine to straight stitching and thread with matching thread.*

2 *On a single thickness of fabric stay stitch adjacent to the sewing line on the seam allowance side. Follow the direction of sewing indicated on the paper pattern.*

3 *When stay stitching is completed construct the garment as required, removing stay stitching later if necessary.*

Sewer's tip

On very fine or sheer fabric a tear-away stabilizer might be useful. It will handle better when sewing in a single thickness and can be torn away later.

GARMENT/PROJECT

Use stay stitching on the necklines of shirts and dresses, princess line dresses, or on other curved seams. It is not necessary on straight seams.

FABRIC

Some stretch fabrics may benefit from stay stitching. Use it on areas of a garment, in any fabric, where the grain is unstable.

NOTIONS AND STITCH SIZE

Use a needle suitable for the fabric weight and type (pages 14–15). Stitch length should be 12 stitches per 1 in. (2.5mm).

ALTERNATIVE

Use a running stitch carried out by hand.

PRESSING AND FINISHING

No special care is needed.

Serger/overlocking stitches

Originating from the manufacture of high-street clothing, sergers are used widely in the home today. Although their primary application is for seaming and neatening edges, these stitches are suited to other, more decorative tasks as well. This chapter provides a guide to adjusting the tensions and selecting the threads for the different serger stitches.

Narrow serging

Narrow serging uses three threads
—one in the needle (in the right-
hand position) and two in the
loopers. It is used for neatening
finished edges and making seams.

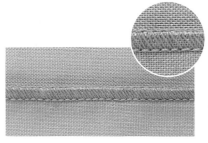

1 *Remove the left
needle. Thread the right
needle and two loopers and
ensure the thread tensions
are balanced. Test the stitch
on spare fabric first.*

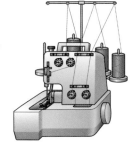

2 *Feed the fabric
under the presser foot and
serge. For neatening edges,
feed the raw edge next to
the blade so that it does
not cut off any fabric. For
seaming, feed the raw edge
in, following the guide on
the foot plate to include the
seam allowance.*

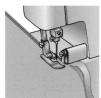

GARMENT/PROJECT

Use on any garment for neatening
raw edges or creating seams and
finishing in one step. Three-thread
narrow serging can also be used for
finishing hems.

FABRIC

Use for stretch, knitted fabrics in light
and medium weights mainly. It can
also be used for woven fabric.

NOTIONS AND STITCH SIZE

Use the right needle only. Choose a
needle according to the type and
weight of fabric (see pages 14–15).
Use a shorter stitch length for lighter
weight material.

ALTERNATIVE

Hand—use a back stitch and an
overcast stitch. Sewing machine—
there are pre-programmed serger
stitches on some machines, although
the excess fabric will need to be cut
away with scissors. Some machines
have a serger foot which helps when
guiding the fabric through.

PRESSING AND FINISHING

Iron serged hems flat. Iron serged
seams to one side when completed.

Sewer's tips

Where a very durable seam is required, a four-thread
seam should be used.

If there is no guide for seam widths, place masking
tape on the serger foot plate and mark your
own guidelines.

Wide serging—THREE THREAD

Wide serging with three threads uses the left needle and the two loopers. Use it for neatening finished edges and for making seams.

Reverse

Front

1
Remove the right needle. Thread the left needle and two loopers, and ensure the thread tensions are balanced. Test the stitch on spare fabric first.

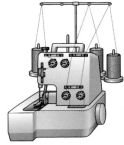

2
Feed the fabric under the presser foot and serge. For neatening edges, feed the raw edge next to the blade so that it does not cut off any fabric. For seaming, feed the raw edge in, following the guide on the foot plate to include the seam allowance.

GARMENT/PROJECT

Use on any garment for neatening raw edges or creating seams and finishing in one step.

FABRIC

Use for stretch, knitted fabrics in medium and heavier weights mainly. It can also be used for woven cloth.

NOTIONS AND STITCH SIZE

Use the left needle only. Choose a needle according to the type and weight of fabric (see page 14). Use longer stitches for thicker cloth.

ALTERNATIVE

Hand—use a back stitch and an overcast stitch. Sewing machine—there are pre-programmed serger stitches on some machines, although the excess fabric will need to be cut away with scissors. Some machines have a serger foot which helps when guiding the fabric through.

PRESSING AND FINISHING

Iron serged hems flat. Iron serged seams to one side when completed.

Sewer's tips

If there is no guide for seam widths, place masking tape on the serger foot plate and mark your own guidelines.

Where a very durable seam is required a four-thread seam should be used (see page 66) as the fourth thread gives extra strength.

Wide serging—FOUR THREAD

Wide serging with four threads uses both the needles and the two loopers. Use it for making seams where a strong, stable finish is required.

Reverse

Front

1 *With both needles in place, thread the needles and loopers and ensure the tension is balanced. Test the stitch on spare fabric.*

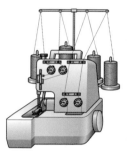

2 *Feed the fabric under the presser foot and serge. If neatening edges, feed the raw edge next to the blade so that it does not cut off any fabric. For seaming, feed the raw edge in following the guide on the foot plate to include the seam allowance.*

GARMENT/PROJECT

Use on any garment for creating strong, stable seams and finishing in one step. It can be used as a neatening stitch but only on heavier, thicker fabrics.

FABRIC

Use for woven fabrics in medium and heavier weights mainly.

NOTIONS AND STITCH SIZE

Use both needles. Choose the same needle for left and right positions, and choose according to the type and weight of fabric (see pages 14–15).

ALTERNATIVE

Hand—use a back stitch and an overcast stitch. Sewing machine—there are pre-programmed serger stitches on some machines, although the excess fabric will need to be cut away with scissors. Some machines have a serger foot which helps when guiding the fabric through.

PRESSING AND FINISHING

Iron serged hems flat. Iron serged seams to one side when completed.

Sewer's tip

If there is no guide for seam widths, place masking tape on the serger foot plate and mark your own guidelines.

Flatlock—TWO THREAD

Flatlock stitch gives a decorative seam finish with loops on one side and ladder stitch on the other. Two-thread flatlocking can only be carried out on models where one of the loopers is blocked, enabling a needle and one looper to create the stitches.

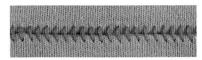

Ladder

Loops

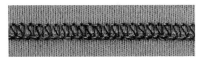

1
Remove one of the needles (depending on whether a wide or narrow effect is required). Thread up according to the manual instructions, as these may differ between machines.

2
Loosen the needle and looper tension

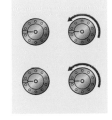

3
For loops on the surface of the seam, feed the fabric through with wrong sides together. For a ladder stitch, put right sides together. Feed through the machine to trim off any excess seam allowance.

4
When completed, pull across the seam until the fabric lies flat and the stitches lie neatly over the join in the fabrics.

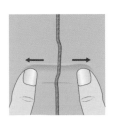

GARMENT/PROJECT

Use flatlocking to make decorative seams for knitted or stretchy garments and sportswear. Use it where a flat finish is needed.

FABRIC

Use for stretch fabrics. Decorative threads can also be used in the loopers.

NOTIONS AND STITCH SIZE

Choose a needle according to the type and weight of fabric (see pages 14–15). A ball point needle is best when stretch fabric is being sewn.

ALTERNATIVE

Hand—overcasting (see page 37). Sewing machine—trim the seam allowance and use a zigzag stitch across the seam edges. This will give a similar effect but will not have the strength of a flatlocked seam.

PRESSING AND FINISHING

Pull across the seam when completed, then iron to flatten the seam.

Flatlock—THREE THREAD

Three-thread flatlocking can be carried out on some models using one needle and two loopers to create the stitches.

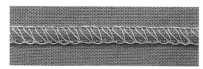

Loops

Ladder

1 *Remove one of the needles, depending on whether a wide or narrow effect is required. Thread up according to the manual instructions (threading differs from machine to machine).*

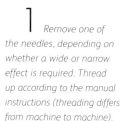

2 *Loosen the needle tension, tighten the lower looper tension, and loosen the upper looper tension.*

3 *For loops on the surface of the seam, feed the fabric through with wrong sides together. For a ladder stitch, put right sides together. Feed through the machine to trim off any excess seam allowance.*

4 *When the seam is completed, gently pull across it until the fabric lies flat and the stitches lie neatly over the join in the fabrics.*

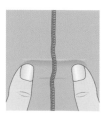

GARMENT/PROJECT

Use flatlocking to make decorative seams for knitted or stretchy garments and sportswear. Use it where a flat finish is needed.

FABRIC

Use for stretch fabrics. Decorative threads can also be used in the loopers.

NOTIONS AND STITCH SIZE

Choose a needle according to the type and weight of fabric (see pages 14–15). A ball point needle is best when stretch fabric is being sewn.

ALTERNATIVE

Hand—overcasting (see page 37). Sewing machine—trim the seam allowance and sew with a zigzag stitch across the seam edges. This will give a similar effect but will not have the strength of a flatlocked seam.

PRESSING AND FINISHING

Pull across the seam when completed, then iron to flatten the seam.

Rolled hem

A serged rolled hem makes a very light, neat edge. It curls the edge of the fabric under and encases the edge with thread. Used with decorative thread or wooly nylon, attractive finishes can be created.

Edge

Seam

1 Remove the left needle, and thread up and shorten stitch length. This will increase thread coverage. Thread up loopers. Depending on the serger model it may be necessary to change the foot or adjust the machine to carry out the rolled hem stitch; check the manual for details.

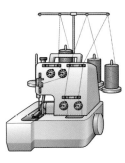

2 Tighten lower looper thread tension. Loosen upper looper tension. Loosen needle tension. Test on scraps and adjust to ensure the result is suitable for the fabric.

3 Hold the chain of threads behind the needle and, with right side uppermost, feed the fabric under the foot, trimming off the excess with the blade. Support the fabric in front of and behind the needle while sewing.

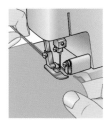

GARMENT/PROJECT

Use a serged rolled hem for hems and frilled edges of garments but also for scarves, table linen, lingerie, and seams on a lightweight sheer fabric.

FABRIC

Use on light- to mediumweight fabric. Use it to hem cottons, silks, and sheer fabrics, and for seams in chiffon or organza.

NOTIONS AND STITCH SIZE

Use a suitable needle for the cloth (generally a size 9 or 11). Use a short stitch for rolled hemming.

ALTERNATIVE

Some sergers have a two-thread rolled hem facility. Hand—use a hand-stitched rolled hem (see page 146). Sewing machine—use a rolled hem foot attachment. It helps to fold the fabric edge over and under the needle. A straight stitch or zigzag can be used to hold the hem in place.

PRESSING AND FINISHING

Iron gently across the rolled edge. Where the rolled hem is off the fabric grain take care not to stretch the hem and make it curl. Spray starch can help.

Picot edge

A picot edge is similar to a rolled hem, but as there is less thread coverage a less stiff effect is created. Use embroidery floss or metallic thread for a decorative finish.

1 *Remove the left needle and thread up. Thread up loopers. Lengthen the stitch length. Depending on the serger model, it may be necessary to change the foot or adjust the machine to carry out the rolled hem stitch. Check the manual for details.*

2 *Adjust thread tensions. Tighten lower looper thread tension. Loosen upper thread and needle thread tension. Test on spare fabric and adjust to ensure the result is suitable for the fabric.*

3 *Hold the chain of threads behind the needle, and with right side uppermost feed the fabric under the foot, trimming off the excess with the blade. Support the fabric in front of and behind the needle whilst sewing.*

GARMENT/PROJECT

Use a picot edge for scarves and hems on soft fabric, for lingerie, and frilled hems.

FABRIC

Use on light- to mediumweight fabric that has a soft feel and where a rolled edge would create a stiffer edge. Use it to hem soft cottons, silks, and chiffons.

NOTIONS AND STITCH SIZE

Use a suitable needle for the cloth. Generally, since fine, lightweight fabrics use picot edgings, a size 9 or 11 will be suitable. Use a long stitch.

ALTERNATIVE

Some sergers have a two-thread picot edge facility. Hand—use a hand-stitched rolled hem (see page 146). Sewing machine—use a rolled hem foot attachment and a long zigzag stitch over the folded edge

PRESSING AND FINISHING

Iron gently across the picot edge. Where the picot edge is off the fabric grain care must be taken not to stretch the edge to make it curl. Spray starch can sometimes prevent this.

Lettuce edge

A lettuce edge hem is possible on a knitted fabric or on a bias-cut fabric. It is produced by sewing a serged rolled hem whilst stretching the fabric to create a curly edge.

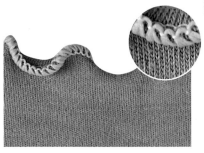

1 *Remove the left needle, and thread up and shorten stitch length to increase thread coverage. Thread up loopers. It may be necessary to change the foot or adjust the machine for rolled hem stitch. (Check the manual.) The differential feed should be off or at a minimum*

2 *Adjust thread tensions. Tighten lower looper thread tension. Loosen upper thread and needle thread tension. Test on spare fabric and adjust before beginning.*

3 *With right side uppermost, feed the fabric under the foot, trimming off excess with the blade. Pull the fabric in front of the needle to make extra stitches in the length and produce the curl in the fabric.*

GARMENT/PROJECT

Use a lettuce hem for little girls' dresses, cuffs, and frills, and for finishing ladies' T-shirts and blouses.

FABRIC

Use on light- to medium-weight fabric. Use it to hem knitted cottons as well as silk, chiffon, or organza.

NOTIONS AND STITCH SIZE

Use a suitable needle for the cloth. As lettuce edge is normally used for light fabric, a size 9 or 11 will be suitable. Use a short stitch and pull the fabric whilst sewing.

ALTERNATIVE

Using the above method, sew over fishing line (minimum breaking strain 18 lb. [80g]) to create a flouncy fishing line edge. Sew as for a rolled hem over the line, leaving excess line at the end of the hem. Pull the line to create waves rather than small curls in the hem edge. This is more suitable for ladies' evening wear than children's clothing.

PRESSING AND FINISHING

Iron gently without flattening the curled edge.

Decorative stitches

Whether made by hand or machine, there is a broad range of decorative stitches to suit every style. It's possible to achieve stunning results, and the diagrams and details in the following pages will show you how. Use the advice on fabric, thread, and needle choice to make sewing easier, and follow the alternatives given for new, creative ideas.

Tucks

Tucks are stitched folds of fabric. They can be sewn singly or in multiples to reduce fullness or to add decoration. They can vary in width; very narrow tucks are called pin tucks (see page 74).

1 *Transfer the pattern markings and press the folds into the fabric. If not using a commercial pattern, make a template in card to use as a guide.*

2 *Set the sewing machine for straight stitch, or a decorative stitch if preferred.*

3 *Sew all tucks in the same direction. Finish thread ends by threading them on to a needle and securing on the wrong side.*

GARMENT/PROJECT

Tucks are used to distribute fullness instead of gathers or darts. Use them at the waist of pants or skirts, on a bodice or yoke, or at the cuff or shoulder on sleeves. Use tucks for lingerie and for decorating cushions.

FABRIC

Use for light- and mediumweight cottons, sheer organdie, or chiffon and fine wool.

NOTIONS AND STITCH SIZE

Use a fine needle size 9 or 11 and a shorter stitch length.

ALTERNATIVE

Tucks can be created by hand or machine. Try a decorative stitch to make them more interesting.

PRESSING AND FINISHING

Tucks should not be pressed flat. Iron on a thick blanket and place a piece of paper under each one while pressing.

Sewer's tip

Use the guides on the foot plate to keep tucks neat and even. If there are no guides, use tape stuck in place instead.

Pin tucks

Tucks are stitched folds of fabric. Pin tucks are very fine and are normally sewn in multiples to create a delicate effect.

1 *Transfer the pattern markings and press the folds into the fabric. If not using a commercial pattern, make a template in card to use as a guide.*

2 *Set the sewing machine for straight stitch and sew ¹⁄₁₆ in. (0.1cm) from the fold to make each tuck. For corded tucks, insert a fine cord in the fold and sew next to it.*

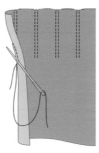

3 *Sew all tucks in the same direction. Finish thread ends by threading on to a needle and securing them on the wrong side.*

GARMENT/PROJECT

Use pin tucks as a delicate finish on children's wear, lingerie, or on bodices and yokes of dresses and blouses. Pin tucks can be used to add texture to cushions and bags.

FABRIC

Use fine, lightweight cotton and silk fabrics.

NOTIONS AND STITCH SIZE

Use a fine needle size 9 or 11 and a small stitch of between 12 and 14 stitches per 1 in. (2.5cm).

ALTERNATIVE

Pin tucks can be created by hand or machine. Try using a zigzag stitch to make them more interesting. The stitches lie over each pin tuck as a row of crosses, especially attractive if using a metallic thread.

PRESSING AND FINISHING

Press very lightly from the wrong side with a thick blanket beneath.

Twin needle tucks

With the appearance of pin tucks, twin needle tucks are created with a twin needle sewing from the surface of the fabric.

1 *Mark the position of the tucks carefully.*

2 *Replace the needle with a twin needle and thread accordingly. Check the manual for specific instructions.*

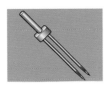

3 *For best results fit a pin tuck foot to the machine. This acts as a guide and arranges the tucks evenly.*

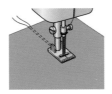

4 *Sew all tucks in the same direction, and sew in loose threads on the wrong side to secure.*

Sewer's tips

Corded tucks can be created by feeding a cord through the machine, or by threading cord through the threads on the wrong side.

Sometimes it helps to tighten the upper thread slightly.

GARMENT/PROJECT

Use twin needle tucks as a delicate finish on children's wear, lingerie, or on bodices and yokes of dresses and blouses. Use to add texture to cushions, bed linen, tablewear, and bags.

FABRIC

Use fine, lightweight fabrics with a smooth surface. Use on mediumweight fabric with a wider twin needle.

NOTIONS AND STITCH SIZE

Use a twin needle. They vary in width from $\frac{1}{16}$ to $\frac{1}{4}$ in. (0.1 to 0.6cm), but not all machines can take a $\frac{1}{4}$ in. (0.6cm) wide twin needle. Use a short stitch of between 12 and 14 stitches per 1 in. (2.5cm) unless working on a heavier weight fabric.

ALTERNATIVE

Pin tucks (see page 74).

PRESSING AND FINISHING

Press very lightly from the wrong side with a thick blanket below.

Attaching lace

Lace can be attached to fabric by machine to add decoration to a bodice or make an attractive hem. A simple zigzag stitch can be used, but a decorative stitch can add interest and texture.

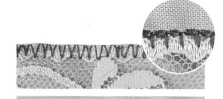

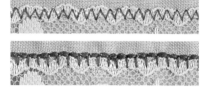

1 *Select a suitable stitch, for example zigzag, blanket, or a similar wide decorative stitch.*

2 *Place lace with the right side uppermost on top of the fabric close to and overlapping the edge. Pin and baste in place.*

3 *Use the inner edge of the lace as a guide and sew over the lace, attaching it to the fabric below.*

4 *Trim away excess fabric below the lace.*

GARMENT/PROJECT

Use either method to attach lace to delicate lingerie, baby clothing, and bed linen.

FABRIC

Use either method for all types of fabric except those which fray badly.

NOTIONS AND STITCH SIZE

Use a suitable needle for the fabric (see pages 14–15). Choose a wide stitch to trap the threads of the fabric, such as zigzag ⅛–¼ in. (3–6mm) wide and approximately ¹⁄₁₆ in. (1mm) in length.

ALTERNATIVE

Use hand overcasting or a three-thread serger stitch rather than a zigzag. Or lap the lace over the fabric edge, zigzag together, and cut the excess lace and fabric away.

PRESSING AND FINISHING

Trim away excess fabric then press on a soft surface using a pressing cloth to protect the surface of the work.

Hem stitch—PULLED THREAD WORK

Pulled or drawn thread work was traditionally used for table linen, handkerchiefs, and bedding. Hem stitch, or spoke stitch, forms a border along one edge of the drawn threads.

1 *Prepare the fabric by removing threads from the weave parallel to the edge. Fold the hem up to the wrong side. Secure the thread end on the wrong side on the left at the start of the work.*

2 *Count three threads (or number required) to the right and take the needle behind and to the left of these, pulling them together.*

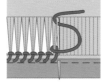

3 *Take the needle to the right of the bundle, taking a small stitch over the edge, catching the hem in the process.*

4 *Repeat steps 2 and 3, gathering regular bundles of threads and stitching the hem in place at the same time.*

Sewer's tip

When complete, neaten the upper edge of the band of drawn threads in the same way (there will not be a hem to catch on the upper edge). This is called ladder hem stitch.

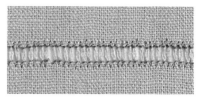

GARMENT/PROJECT

 Pulled or drawn thread work is used to hem handkerchiefs, tablecloths, or bed linen.

FABRIC

 Loosely woven linen where the threads can be withdrawn easily.

NOTIONS AND STITCH SIZE

 Use a tapestry needle and thread of a similar color and thickness to the thread drawn from the fabric. Stitch size will be determined by the number of threads being bundled.

ALTERNATIVE

 A similar effect to pulled thread work can be achieved on a sewing machine with a wing needle.

PRESSING AND FINISHING

 Iron lightly.

Zigzag hem stitch—PULLED THREAD WORK

Threads from the fabric are pulled from the weave and the remaining threads are sewn together to form a decorative finish. Zigzag hem stitch groups bundles of the threads in a zigzag fashion.

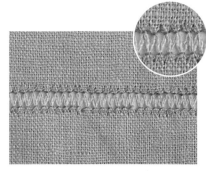

1 *Prepare the fabric by removing threads from the weave (either warp or weft) parallel to the edge. Fold the hem up to the wrong side so that the edge meets the edge of the band of drawn threads. Secure the thread end on the wrong side on the left at the start of the work.*

2 *Neaten the lower edge with a hem stitch (see page 77), bundling the threads in groups of four or six (an even number is required).*

3 *Neaten the upper edge with a hem stitch, splitting each bundle in half and grouping two halves together.*

4 *When completed, a zigzag effect is produced.*

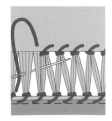

GARMENT/PROJECT

Pulled or drawn thread work is used to hem handkerchiefs, tablecloths, or bed linen.

FABRIC

Loosely woven linen where the threads can be withdrawn easily.

NOTIONS AND STITCH SIZE

Use a tapestry needle and thread of a similar color and thickness to the thread drawn from the fabric. Stitch size will be determined by the number of threads being bundled.

ALTERNATIVE

A similar effect to pulled thread work can be achieved on a sewing machine with a wing needle.

PRESSING AND FINISHING

Iron lightly.

Double hem stitch—PULLED THREAD WORK

Pulled thread work creates an open embroidered effect. For double hem stitch, two bands of threads are removed and the area between is stitched over.

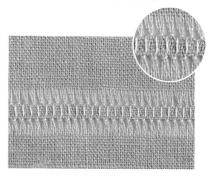

1 *Prepare the fabric by removing a band of threads from the weave. Leave the same number of threads in place, then remove the next band.*

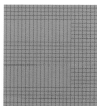

2 *Start on the right at the top of the middle band. Take the needle straight down over the front of the middle band and between the loose threads. Pick up the next four loose threads to the left, then go back over them and down between the threads.*

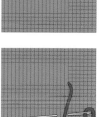

3 *Bring the needle back up on the upper band, four loose threads to the left.*

4 *Take the needle back over and round these four loose threads, bringing the needle back up at the same point. Continue bundling the threads.*

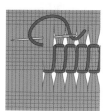

GARMENT/PROJECT

Pulled or drawn thread work is used to hem handkerchiefs, tablecloths, or bed linen.

FABRIC

Loosely and evenly woven linen where the threads can be withdrawn easily.

NOTIONS AND STITCH SIZE

Use a blunt tapestry needle and thread of a similar color and thickness to the thread drawn from the fabric. Stitch size will be determined by the number of threads being bundled.

ALTERNATIVE

A similar effect to pulled thread work can be achieved on a sewing machine with a wing needle.

PRESSING AND FINISHING

Iron lightly.

Knotted hem stitch—PULLED THREAD WORK

Threads from the fabric are pulled from the weave and the remaining threads are sewn together by knotting them in bundles.

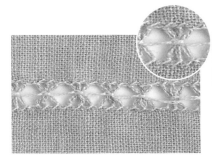

1 *Prepare the fabric by removing a band of threads.*

2 *Finish the upper and lower edges with ladder hem stitch (see page 77).*

3 *Secure the thread end on the right in the middle of the band of thread bundles. Form a loop with the thread over the first three bundles (or required number). Take the needle under the bundles from right to left and through the loop placed on top. Pull to create a knot.*

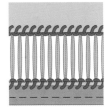

4 *Repeat step 3 to make a row of knotted bundles across the work.*

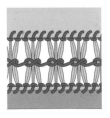

GARMENT/PROJECT

Pulled or drawn thread work is used to hem handkerchiefs, tablecloths, or bed linen.

FABRIC

Loosely and evenly woven linen where the threads can be withdrawn easily.

NOTIONS AND STITCH SIZE

Use a blunt tapestry needle and thread of a similar color and thickness to the thread drawn from the fabric. Stitch size will be determined by the number of threads being bundled.

ALTERNATIVE

A similar effect to pulled thread work can be achieved on a sewing machine with a wing needle.

PRESSING AND FINISHING

Iron lightly.

Twisted hem stitch—PULLED THREAD WORK

Pulled or drawn thread work creates an open embroidered effect. Threads from the fabric are pulled from the weave and the remaining threads bundled and twisted together by stitching.

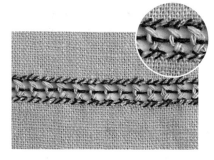

1 *Prepare the fabric by removing a band of threads.*

2 *Finish the upper and lower edges with ladder hem stitch.*

3 *Secure the thread on the right in the middle of the thread bundles. Pass the needle over the first two bundles. Insert the needle under the threads from left to right, picking up the left bundle and going over the right one. Twist the needle downward, making the left bundle cross over the right one.*

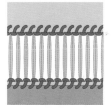

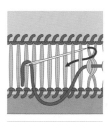

4 *Bring the needle up again and work the next two bundles in the same way.*

GARMENT/PROJECT

Pulled or drawn thread work is used to hem handkerchiefs, tablecloths, or bed linen.

FABRIC

Loosely and evenly woven linen where the threads can be withdrawn easily.

NOTIONS AND STITCH SIZE

Use a blunt tapestry needle and thread of a similar color and thickness to the thread drawn from the fabric. Stitch size will be determined by the number of threads being bundled.

ALTERNATIVE

A similar effect to pulled thread work can be achieved on a sewing machine with a wing needle.

PRESSING AND FINISHING

Iron lightly.

Pin stitch—DRAWN FABRIC WORK

Drawn fabric work is achieved by pulling threads in a fabric apart or together to create pattern and texture. Threads are not withdrawn as they are in pulled or drawn thread work. Pin stitch is used as a border or hem.

1 *Working from the right, pass the needle down and under three (or number required) threads, bringing the needle up to the surface.*

2 *Take the needle back over these threads and down through the same position as before. Bring the needle up again at the end of the stitch just above the sewing line, and pull slightly to draw the fabric threads together.*

3 *Pass the needle back down directly below this, on the sewing line, and continue to pull bundles of threads together along the sewing line.*

GARMENT/PROJECT

Drawn fabric work is generally used for table linen and bedding.

FABRIC

Use loosely and evenly woven linen and cotton.

NOTIONS AND STITCH SIZE

Use a blunt tapestry needle and thread of a similar color and thickness to the thread of the fabric. Stitch size will be determined by the number of threads being pulled together.

ALTERNATIVE

A similar effect to drawn fabric work can be achieved on a sewing machine with a wing needle.

PRESSING AND FINISHING

Iron lightly.

Punch stitch—DRAWN FABRIC WORK

Drawn fabric work is achieved by pulling threads in a fabric apart or together to create pattern and texture. Threads are not withdrawn as they are in pulled or drawn thread work. Punch stitch is used as a filling stitch for embroidery.

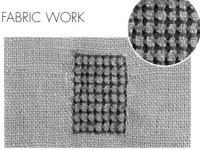

1
Working in a grid, start from the right and make two vertical stitches pulling four (or number required) threads together.

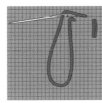

2
Count four threads to the left and make two more vertical stitches parallel to the first. Continue across the work.

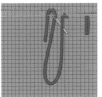

3
Make a second row (and subsequent rows) of stitches immediately below the first.

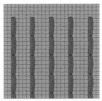

4
Complete the grid by making rows of horizontal stitches in between.

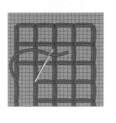

GARMENT/PROJECT

Drawn fabric work is generally used for table linen. Punch stitch is a filling stitch for embroidery.

FABRIC

Use loosely and evenly woven linen and cotton.

NOTIONS AND STITCH SIZE

Use a blunt tapestry needle and thread of a similar color and thickness to the thread of the fabric. Stitch size will be determined by the number of threads being pulled together.

ALTERNATIVE

A similar effect to drawn fabric work can be achieved on a sewing machine with a wing needle.

PRESSING AND FINISHING

Iron lightly.

Smocking

Smocking is an embroidery style sewn on to a base of gathers. Although traditionally worked on farm laborers' smocks, it is now used for children's and ladies' clothing. There are many types of smocking stitches that are selected and combined to form a design. The finished result has a degree of stretch.

GARMENT/PROJECT

Use machine smocking for children's clothes, bodices of evening dresses, bags, and cushions.

FABRIC

Use light- to mediumweight fabrics with a smooth surface, for example cotton lawn, silk broadcloth, and fine wool. Fabrics made from natural fibers are easier to work with than man-made or synthetic ones.

NOTIONS AND STITCH SIZE

For hand smocking, use an embroidery needle with a large enough eye to take the embroidery floss being used. Use a machine embroidery needle for machine smocking.

ALTERNATIVE

Hand or machine.

PRESSING AND FINISHING

Do not flatten the tucks or the embroidery with the iron. If necessary, press very lightly from the wrong side with a blanket beneath.

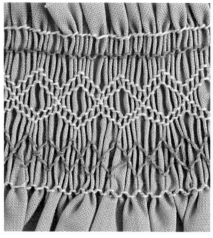

Hand smocking

Machine smocking

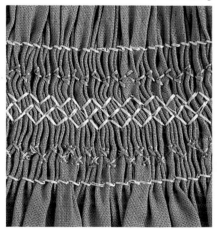

Preparation

To prepare the fabric for smocking it must be gathered up into fine tucks. This can be carried out with a "pleater" or sewn by hand. Sew several rows of regular gathering stitches from the wrong side of the fabric. Pull these up to create a block of tucks and smock from the right side of the cloth.

HAND SMOCKING

The design is normally bordered with outline stitches such as stem stitch or cable stitch which have a firm control of the pleats, and loose control stitches such as trellis, wave, diamond, and others forming the bands in between.

Stem stitch

1 *Work from left to right and make each stitch through each pleat. Secure the thread and make a stitch through the pleat on the right, keeping the thread above the needle.*

2 *Make the next stitch in the same way by picking up the pleat on the right, keeping the thread above the needle. Continue creating stem stitches across the length of the work.*

Cable stitch

1 *Work from left to right and make each stitch through each pleat. Secure the thread and make a stitch through the pleat on the right, keeping the thread above the needle.*

2 *Make the second stitch through the next pleat on the right, keeping the thread below the needle.*

3 *The third stitch is created with the thread above the needle. Continue alternating in this way across the length of the work.*

Sewer's tip

Cable stitch can be worked on its own or in multiple rows.

Wave stitch

1 Work from left to right and make each stitch through each pleat. Secure the thread and make a stitch through the pleat on the right, keeping the thread below the needle.

2 Make three or four more stitches in the same way as step 1 to continue the upward direction.

3 Make the next stitch, keeping the thread above the needle, and three or four more like this. These stitches will be in a downward direction. Continue creating stitches to make a wave pattern across the length of the work.

4 Make subsequent rows of stitching in the same way below the first.

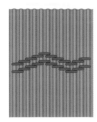

Trellis stitch

1 Make a row of wave stitching following the instructions above.

2 For the second row, start immediately below the first stitch and make the first block of stitches in a downward direction, keeping the thread above the needle.

3 Make the next block of stitches in an upward direction, keeping the thread below the needle.

4 This will create a series of diamonds and subsequent rows will form a trellis design.

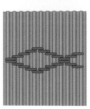

Diamond stitch

1 *Work from left to right and make each stitch through each pleat. Secure the thread and make a stitch through the pleat on the right, keeping the thread below the needle.*

2 *Make a diagonal stitch upward through the next pleat followed by a horizontal stitch, keeping the thread above the needle.*

3 *Make a diagonal stitch downward and follow it with a horizontal stitch, keeping the thread below the needle. Continue creating these stitches to the end of the row.*

4 *The row below is worked in the same way, mirroring the first row to create diamonds across the work.*

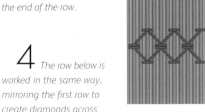

MACHINE SMOCKING

As sewing machines have developed over recent years the opportunity to smock by machine has evolved. There are many pre-programmed stitches suitable for machine smocking, and some smocking patterns have been produced on disc for the more advanced computerized machines.

1 *Prepare the fabric as for hand smocking and place a fusible tear-away or wash-away stabilizer on the wrong side.*

2 *Consider the stitches available on the sewing machine and choose the design and order of stitches required.*

3 *Using the lines of gathering stitches as a guide machine each row, starting from the top and working down.*

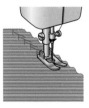

4 *When the machine stitches are in place, remove all the gathering stitches and complete the garment.*

Beading

Sewing beads and sequins to an embroidered picture or garment will add texture and sparkle, and make it special. Although generally sewn on by hand, linear beads can be attached by machine or with the use of a hook.

GARMENT/PROJECT

Beads and sequins can be added to ladies' evening wear and girls' party dresses around necklines, cuffs, and hemlines. They are also popular on bags and cushions.

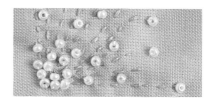

FABRIC

Add beads to any fabric.

NOTIONS AND STITCH SIZE

For hand beading use a beading needle which is very long and fine. For Tambour beading use a Tambour hook which is like a very fine crochet hook. For beads sewn on with a sewing machine use a standard needle and a beading foot which allows the beads to pass under the foot. The machine should be set at a wide, long zigzag to cover the beads.

ALTERNATIVE

Buy already beaded fabric and incorporate into the design.

PRESSING AND FINISHING

Do not use an iron as this will tarnish or melt beads and sequins.

SEWING SEQUINS AND BEADS BY HAND

Preparation

Place the fabric to be worked on in a frame or hoop.

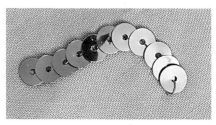

Individual sequins

1 *Secure the thread and bring it through at the sequin position. Bring the needle through the hole in the sequin and across the surface, taking it down at the edge.*

2 *Bring the needle back up through the hole in the sequin and take it down again at a different point on the edge.*

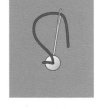

3 *Use as many stitches as desired to attach the sequin, bearing in mind that the greater the thread coverage the less light will be reflected.*

Linear sequins

1 *Secure the thread and bring it through at the sequin position. Bring the needle through the hole in the sequin and across the surface, taking it down at the edge where the next sequin will be applied.*

2 *Bring the needle up along the line of stitching half a sequin's width away. Place the next sequin half to overlap the first one. Take the needle back over the second sequin and down through the hole.*

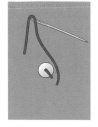

3 *Pull the thread through and adjust the sequin to lie half over the previous one. Continue with back stitches, threading the sequins one at a time, each covering half of the previous one.*

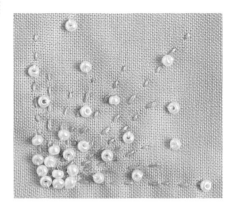

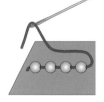

Individual beads

1 Secure the thread in the position of the first bead. Pass the needle through the hole in the bead and back through under the bead to the wrong side. For individual beads secure the thread end on the wrong side.

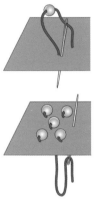

2 For a row or cluster of beads, bring the needle up to the surface at the next bead position and repeat.

Linear beads

1 Gather beads on to a length of thread. Lay the threaded beads on the surface of the fabric and sew in place with a second thread.

2 Start from one end and catch the thread with stitches between the beads for the length of the work.

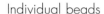

Sewer's tip

Secure threads at the start and finish of the work to ensure the beads do not fall off. Use a double thread for extra strength if fine enough.

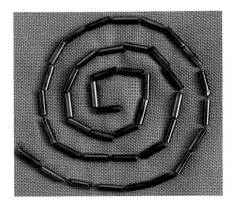

Tambour beadwork

Similar to sewing on a threaded length of beads, this method uses a fine hook instead of a needle.

SEWING BEADS AND SEQUINS WITH A MACHINE

A string of beads or pearls can be sewn to a fabric using a beading foot, and sequins can be attached with a sequin or ribbon foot. This feeds the beads and sequins through while the machine zigzags over them in a similar way to couching.

1
Place the fabric into a hoop to hold it taut.

2
From the wrong side, pass the hook through the fabric. Pick up the thread before the first bead, pull the end through and make a loop.

3
Pass the hook down through the fabric and pick up the thread on the other side of the first bead. Pull the thread back through the fabric and the loop already around the needle as if creating a chain. Repeat along the length of the beads.

1
Fit the beading (or ribbon) foot to the machine and set the stitch to zigzag.

2
With the fabric positioned at the start and the presser foot raised, feed the beads/sequins under the foot and sew slowly, guiding the work along the sewing line.

3
Secure the threads at the end of the work and cut off any excess beads/sequins.

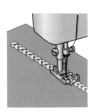

Insertion stitches

Insertion stitches are used to join two pieces of fabric and create a decorative open work seam or hem. It is also called faggoting.

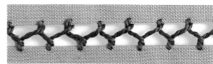

Insertion stitch

1 *Starting on the left on the upper edge, bring the thread through from the inside through the fold.*

GARMENT/PROJECT

Use insertion stitches for lingerie, attaching lace, on the hem of a dress, or as a decorative seam. Use it for bed linen or for detail on drapes.

FABRIC

Use on light- to mediumweight fabric, for example, cotton lawn, linen, or silk dupion.

2 *Take the needle through the fold on the lower edge from front to back, a stitch length to the right, keeping the thread on the right.*

NOTIONS AND STITCH SIZE

Use a crewel needle with a large enough eye to take the embroidery floss used.

ALTERNATIVE

Pulled thread work has a similar appearance to insertion stitching or faggoting. Use a wing needle on a sewing machine to get a similar effect.

3 *Take the needle through the upper fold from front to back, a stitch length to the right, keeping the thread to the right.*

PRESSING AND FINISHING

Use a pressing cloth to protect the surface of the work.

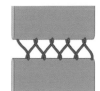

4 *Repeat with these two stitches catching the edges alternatively with a twisted stitch.*

Preparation

Before starting to sew, neaten the edges with a very narrow hem or join folds of fabric. Baste to graph paper, positioning the fabric edges approximately ¼ in. (0.6cm) apart. The graph paper will ensure stitches are even and regular.

Knotted insertion stitch

1 *Starting on the left on the upper edge, bring the thread through from the inside through the fold.*

2 *Take the needle through the fold on the lower edge from front to back, a stitch length to the right, keeping the thread on the right. Pass the needle under the threads from left to right. Loop the thread over the threads and pass the needle through the loop.*

3 *Take the needle through the upper fold. Pass the needle under the threads from left to right. Loop the thread over the threads and pass the needle through the loop.*

4 *Continue with these two stitches, making knots on alternate edges.*

Bar stitch

1 *Start on the upper edge on the left. Bring the needle through the top edge, then take a stitch through the fold on the lower edge from front to back directly below.*

2 *Wind the needle round the stitch, joining the two edges. The distance between the edges will determine the number of times. This creates a corded effect.*

3 *Take the needle back through the upper edge by the first stitch then through the upper edge to the start position of the next stitch, one stitch length to the right.*

4 *Continue creating the bars to complete the work.*

Cut work

Cut work is an open embroidery, which is stronger than it appears because the buttonhole stitches covering the raw edges of the design give support to the work. The design is cut away after the stitching is complete.

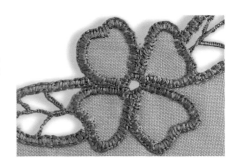

GARMENT/PROJECT

Use cut work to decorate ladies' dresses and shirts. Use on tablecloths and napkins as well as sheets and pillowcases.

FABRIC

Use fabric that is tightly woven and does not fray easily.

NOTIONS AND STITCH SIZE

Use a sharp pointed embroidery needle and stranded embroidery floss or pearl cotton for handmade cut work. Keep the buttonhole stitches close together when covering an edge and spaced slightly further apart for double buttonhole stitch. Use an embroidery needle and machine embroidery floss for machined cut work with a short wide zigzag for the cut edges.

ALTERNATIVE

Hand or machine method.

PRESSING AND FINISHING

Iron lightly from the wrong side when completed.

HANDMADE CUT WORK

Open areas

1 *Transfer the design to the fabric and outline each part of the design to be cut away with a running stitch (see page 28).*

2 *Make buttonhole stitches over the running stitch to cover the edges which will be cut away.*

3 *Using small sharp-pointed scissors trim the excess fabric away from the buttonhole-stitched edges.*

Cut work bars

1 *Sew three or four threads in position over the fabric in the design, the length of the required bar.*

2 *Start from one end and form buttonhole stitches around the strands of thread. Continue until the thread strands are completely covered. Secure the thread in the work.*

Double buttonhole stitch

1 *Secure the thread at one end of the sewing line and make a row of buttonhole stitches along the line.*

2 *Make a second row of stitches from the opposite side, filling the gaps left in the first row.*

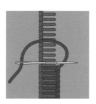

MACHINED CUT WORK

A similar, much more quickly produced effect can be created by machine with a satin stitch using a zigzag stitch.

1 *Baste a tear-away stabilizer to the wrong side and transfer the design to the surface of the fabric.*

2 *With a short straight stitch on the machine and matching thread, sew round the design carefully.*

3 *Set the machine to a short length zigzag to create a satin stitch. Sew over the straight stitches with the zigzag. Using sharp-pointed scissors trim the excess fabric away. Remove the tear-away stabilizer, leaving it under the zigzag stitches.*

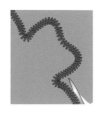

Ribbon embroidery

Sewing with ribbon builds up a design quickly and creates a lovely 3D texture. It is ideal for depicting flowers and leaves.

GARMENT/PROJECT

Ribbon embroidery can be worked on many items, from woven cotton shirts to knitted cardigans and jackets. It can also be used to decorate hats, bags, and cushions.

FABRIC

Most fabrics are suitable for ribbon embroidery, but tightly woven ones may cause more damage to the ribbon as it passes through the cloth. The best ribbons to use are soft, silk ones with no hard edges.

NOTIONS AND STITCH SIZE

A broad tapestry needle makes a hole in the fabric allowing more room for the ribbon and the large eye prevents the ribbon from creasing. Use short lengths of ribbon so that it will not become too damaged whilst passing in and out of the fabric.

ALTERNATIVE

Ribbon can be machined in place using a ribbon foot attachment, but this does not allow the 3D texture created by hand ribbon embroidery.

PRESSING AND FINISHING

Do not iron ribbon work as it will flatten the textured finish.

Preparation

Place the fabric in a hoop to hold it taut. Thread a short length of ribbon through a large-eyed tapestry needle and tie a knot in the end. Sew each stitch as if it was thread, but leave each stitch loose to create the texture. To finish, take the ribbon to the wrong side and cut. Thread up a fine needle with cotton or silk thread and secure the ribbon with this. This reduces any excess bulk.

Padded straight stitch

1 *Thread the ribbon on to the needle and bring it through to the surface at the start of the stitch. Take the needle down through the fabric at the end position of the stitch but leave the stitch slightly loose.*

2 *Make a second stitch directly over the first one. Again, do not pull the ribbon tight but leave it slightly loose to create depth. Finish on the wrong side with a second thread as described above.*

Ribbon stitch

1 Thread the ribbon on to the needle and bring the needle through to the surface at the start of the stitch. Hold the ribbon flat but loosely on the fabric, and take the needle down through the ribbon and the fabric at the end of the stitch.

2 Pull the ribbon almost through, leaving the edges curving at the end of the stitch to look like a simple petal or leaf. Finish on the wrong side with a second thread as described above.

Gathered ribbon

1 Cut a short length of ribbon and sew a running stitch along one edge. Pull up to form gathers and secure.

2 With a second thread (in matching cotton or silk) sew the gathered edge to the fabric in a circle with small stitches. This creates a ribbon rose effect.

Couching

Couching involves sewing over a length of thread or cord, thus holding it in position. It is used for stems of flowers, but several rows can be couched adjacent to each other to fill an area. Stiff metallic threads can be sewn this way.

1 *Secure the thread at the back of the work and bring the needle through at the start of the sewing line. Place the thread or cord on the sewing line and take the needle over it and down into the fabric on the other side.*

2 *Continue making stitches over the thread/cord, working along its length to hold it in place on the sewing line. If the cord has an obvious twist, use diagonal stitches at the same angle as the twist so that they will be concealed in the cord.*

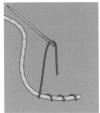

GARMENT/PROJECT

Use this for stems of flowers or smooth curving lines. Use it as a filling stitch with many rows together, or for attaching stiff metal threads or plate.

FABRIC

Use to decorate all fabrics.

NOTIONS AND STITCH SIZE

Use a small hand needle and cotton or silk sewing thread, and straight or diagonal stitches to suit the thread or cord being couched.

ALTERNATIVE

Machine couching is easy to do with a zigzag stitch and a cording foot. The foot guides the cord through the machine in the correct position for the stitches to catch it in place.

PRESSING AND FINISHING

If necessary, iron from the wrong side on a thick, soft surface.

Cretan stitch

Cretan stitch is made in a similar way to herringbone and can be worked open for a textured effect or closed as a filling stitch. It can also be used as an insertion stitch.

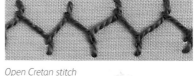

Open Cretan stitch

Closed Cretan stitch

OPEN CRETAN

1 *Work from left to right and use two guidelines to keep stitches even. Bring the needle through to the surface in the center and then take it down on the lower guideline, to the right. Keep the thread above the needle and bring the needle back up directly above this.*

2 *Keep the thread below the needle and take it down through the fabric on the upper guideline. Bring the needle back up to the surface directly below this.*

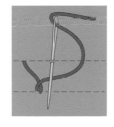

3 *Continue working between the guidelines to complete the row.*

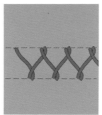

Closed Cretan

The stitches are worked in the same way with more fabric being picked up every stitch and each stitch worked closer together.

GARMENT/PROJECT

Use Cretan stitch for embroidery to depict grasses when open and leaves when closed. It works well as a border and as an insertion stitch.

FABRIC

Use on all embroidery fabrics.

NOTIONS AND STITCH SIZE

Use an embroidery needle to suit the cloth with a large enough eye to take the embroidery floss used.

ALTERNATIVE

Use feather, fly, or herringbone stitch instead of open Cretan, and satin stitch in place of closed Cretan. You can also use sewing machine's pre-programmed decorative stitches.

PRESSING AND FINISHING

Do not flatten embroidery stitches with an iron.

Machine embroidery

Modern sewing machines offer a range of pre-programmed decorative stitches (see below) that can be used in a variety of ways. Use them with machine embroidery floss or metallic threads, and in conjunction with ribbons and cords. Free stitching machine embroidery (see opposite) is also possible and allows more individual creativity.

Suitable for smocking

Sew with a wing needle

Decorative edging

Suitable for smocking

Decorative border

Sew over ribbon

1 *Prepare the machine by lowering or covering the feed dog or teeth and replacing the presser foot with a darning foot. Check the manual for details.*

2 *Thread up the machine with embroidery floss in the needle and the bobbin, and set the machine length and width to "0." Prepare the fabric by placing in a hoop and pulling taut.*

3 *Place the fabric in the hoop under the needle. The raw edges of the fabric should face upward and the smooth hoop downward on the machine bed.*

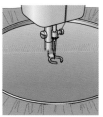

4 *Turn the handle manually and allow the needle to pass into the hoop of fabric and pull up the bobbin thread. Hold on to these thread tails, lower the presser foot, and stitch steadily, moving the hoop slowly to produce small stitches. The stitching can be totally free or guidelines can be drawn with a soluble pen.*

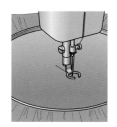

GARMENT/PROJECT

 A panel of a garment, such as a bodice front or yoke, could be embroidered before being made up, but free embroidery is more often used for art. Pre-programmed stitches can be used to decorate cushions, bed linen, and other household items.

FABRIC

 A mediumweight fabric like calico is best, but heavier weights can be used. On lighter-weight fabric a tear-away or wash-away stabilizer is required.

NOTIONS AND STITCH SIZE

 Use embroidery bobbin floss in the bobbin for pre-programmed stitches. For machine embroidery of all types use a size 14 needle. Use a metallic needle for metallic threads as this has a larger hole which prevents the thread from shredding. Stitch length and width should be set at "0" and the hoop moved slowly to achieve small stitches or faster for larger stitches. The needle tension can be loosened if necessary to improve the stitch quality.

ALTERNATIVE

 Hand-embroidered designs or computerized embroidery motifs.

PRESSING AND FINISHING

 Remove any stabilizer if necessary. Do not iron unless essential; if so, iron lightly on the reverse.

Stem stitch

Use stem stitch for curved and straight lines in embroidery. It is used for flower stems, outlines, and for filling when sewn in closely worked rows.

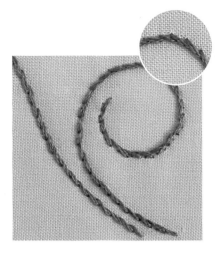

1 *Working from left to right, bring the needle up to the surface on the sewing line to start. Take the needle down, a stitch to the right, and bring it up halfway along and above the previous stitch.*

2 *Take another stitch to the right, bringing the needle back up above the previous stitch as before.*

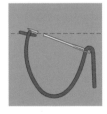

3 *Continue creating stitches in this way.*

GARMENT/PROJECT

Use this as for embroidery or to decorate a garment.

FABRIC

Stem stitch can be worked on all fabrics.

NOTIONS AND STITCH SIZE

Use an embroidery needle to suit the weight of cloth with a large enough eye to take the embroidery floss used. Take smaller stitches on tighter curves to create a smooth line.

ALTERNATIVE

Use back stitch, chain stitch, split stitch, or laced running stitch for a solid line. Use zigzag or couching for a similar effect with the sewing machine.

PRESSING AND FINISHING

Do not flatten embroidery stitches with an iron. If necessary, iron from the wrong side on a thick, soft surface.

Cable stitch

Cable stitch is an embroidery stitch. It is an outline stitch producing a line or border, and is used in smocking.

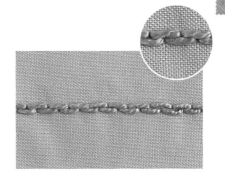

1 *Working from left to right, bring the needle up to the surface on the sewing line to start. Take the needle down, a stitch to the right, and bring it up halfway along and above the previous stitch.*

2 *Take another stitch to the right, bringing the needle back up halfway along the previous stitch as before, but this time below. Continue creating stitches alternating above and below, making two adjacent lines of sewing.*

GARMENT/PROJECT

Use cable stitch for smocking and for embroidery or to decorate a garment.

FABRIC

Cable stitch can be worked on all fabrics.

NOTIONS AND STITCH SIZE

Use an embroidery needle to suit the weight of cloth with a large enough eye to take the embroidery floss used.

ALTERNATIVE

Use back stitch, chain stitch, or laced running stitch for a solid outline or border. Use zigzag stitch for a similar effect with the sewing machine.

PRESSING AND FINISHING

Do not flatten embroidery stitches with an iron. If necessary, iron from the wrong side on a thick, soft surface.

Chain stitch

Use chain stitch for lines in embroidery. It produces quick and effective straight and curved lines. Chain stitch can also be used as a padding stitch below a satin stitch to add depth to a design.

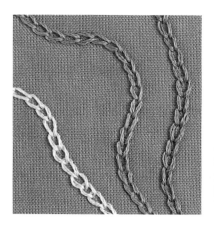

1 *Bring the needle through to the surface at the start of the sewing line. Take the needle back down very close to where it came up, then bring it back up to the surface at the end position of the first stitch. Loop the thread under the point of the needle then pull through. Adjust the stitch to make a neat loop.*

2 *Take the needle back down close to where it came up in the loop and bring it up at the end position of the next stitch. Loop the thread under the point of the needle then pull through.*

3 *Continue to create a chain of links; finish by catching the final loop with a small stitch to ensure the chain does not come undone.*

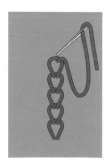

GARMENT/PROJECT

 Use chain stitch for embroidery or to decorate a garment.

FABRIC

 Chain stitch can be worked on all fabrics.

NOTIONS AND STITCH SIZE

 Use an embroidery needle to suit the weight of cloth with a large enough eye to take the embroidery floss used.

ALTERNATIVE

 Use back stitch, stem stitch, or laced running stitch for a solid outline or border. Alternative chain stitches include twisted chain and open chain.

PRESSING AND FINISHING

 Do not flatten embroidery stitches with an iron. If necessary, iron from the wrong side on a thick, soft surface.

Lazy daisy stitch

Lazy daisy stitch or detached chain stitch is a variation of chain stitch where each chain or loop makes a daisy-like petal.

1 *Bring the needle up to the surface at the start of the stitch position. Take the needle back down very close to this.*

2 *Bring the needle back up to the surface at the end position of the stitch. Adjust the stitch to make a neat loop then take a tiny stitch over the loop to hold it in place.*

3 *Make individual stitches, or groups to form petals.*

GARMENT/PROJECT

Use lazy daisy stitch for embroidery, especially flowers, or for decoration on a garment.

FABRIC

Lazy daisy stitch can be worked on all fabrics.

NEEDLE AND STITCH SIZE

Use an embroidery needle to suit the weight of cloth with a large enough eye to take the embroidery floss used.

ALTERNATIVE

To create flowers use satin stitch; some sewing machines may offer a suitable pre-programmed stitch.

PRESSING AND FINISHING

Do not flatten embroidery stitches with an iron. If necessary, iron from the wrong side on a thick, soft surface.

Satin stitch

Satin stitch is created by rows of adjacent straight stitches. It is a filling stitch, often used for petals and leaves. It can be worked on its own or with padding stitches below.

1 *Start at one end of the area to be filled and bring the needle up to the surface at the edge. Sew a straight stitch to reach the opposite edge.*

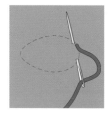

2 *Take the needle down and under the work back to the start of the first stitch, bringing the needle up to the surface next to the first one. Make a second stitch adjacent to the first.*

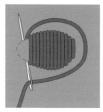

3 *Continue to sew, adjusting the length of the stitch to fit the area to be filled.*

GARMENT/PROJECT

Use satin stitch for embroidery or for decoration on a garment.

FABRIC

Satin stitch can be worked on all fabrics.

NEEDLE AND STITCH SIZE

Use an embroidery needle to suit the weight of cloth with a large enough eye to take the embroidery floss used.

ALTERNATIVE

Use an alternative filling stitch such as long and short stitch, or to create flowers use lazy daisy stitch. Use a short wide zigzag for satin stitch on a sewing machine.

PRESSING AND FINISHING

Do not flatten embroidery stitches with an iron. If necessary, iron from the wrong side on a thick, soft surface.

Sewer's tip

Stitches must be parallel but may be worked horizontally, vertically, or at an angle.

Single satin

Single satin or straight stitches can be made in any direction and sewn singly or in groups to create a design. They can vary in length and be sewn in a regular pattern or in a scattered manner.

1 *Bring the needle up to the surface at the start of the stitch. Take the needle down at the end position of the stitch.*

2 *If the next stitch is close by bring the needle up to the surface at the start of the second stitch and continue; if not, finish the thread on the wrong side.*

Sewer's tip

The stitches should be neither too long nor too loose.

GARMENT/PROJECT

Use single satin or straight stitch for embroidery for flower petals, small stems, or grasses.

FABRIC

Single satin stitch can be worked on all fabrics.

NEEDLE AND STITCH SIZE

Use an embroidery needle to suit the weight of cloth with a large enough eye to take the embroidery floss used.

ALTERNATIVE

Use lazy daisy stitch as an alternative for flowers.

PRESSING AND FINISHING

Do not flatten embroidery stitches with an iron. If necessary, iron from the wrong side on a thick, soft surface.

Split stitch

Similar to stem stitch, split stitch is ideal for lines in embroidery. Suitable for curved and straight lines, it is used for flower stems, outlines, and also for filling when sewn in closely worked rows to give a fine flat surface.

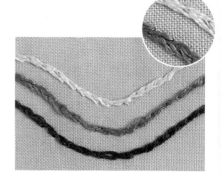

1 *Working from left to right, bring the needle up to the surface on the sewing line to start. Take the needle down, a stitch to the right, and bring it up halfway along the previous stitch through the thread.*

2 *Take another stitch to the right, bringing the needle back up through the previous stitch as before. Continue creating stitches in this way.*

GARMENT/PROJECT

Use this for embroidery or to decorate a garment where straight or curved lines are required.

FABRIC

Split stitch can be worked on all fabrics.

NOTIONS AND STITCH SIZE

Use an embroidery needle to suit the weight of cloth with a large enough eye to take the embroidery floss used.

ALTERNATIVE

Use back stitch, chain stitch, stem stitch, or laced running stitch for a solid line. Use couching for a similar effect with the sewing machine.

PRESSING AND FINISHING

Do not flatten embroidery stitches with an iron. If necessary, iron from the wrong side on a thick, soft surface.

Laced running stitch

Laced running stitch makes a bolder finish and can be sewn in the same or a contrasting color. Use it for edges and borders.

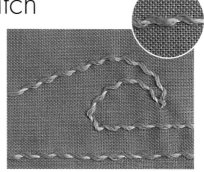

1 *Sew a row of running stitch to prepare.*

2 *Start at one end of the work, and using the back of the needle or a blunt tapestry needle lace the thread in and out of the running stitches. (A sharp point might pick up the fabric or split the thread.)*

GARMENT/PROJECT

Use this for embroidery or to decorate a garment where straight or curved lines are required, or use it as an edge or border.

FABRIC

Laced running stitch can be worked on all fabrics.

NOTIONS AND STITCH SIZE

Use an embroidery needle to suit the weight of cloth with a large enough eye to take the embroidery floss used for the running stitch, but use the back of the needle or a blunt tapestry needle for the lacing.

ALTERNATIVE

Use back stitch, chain stitch, or stem stitch for a solid line or border. Use couching as an alternative machine method.

PRESSING AND FINISHING

Do not flatten embroidery stitches with an iron. If necessary, iron from the wrong side on a thick, soft surface.

Pekinese stitch

Similar to laced running stitch, Pekinese stitch is an embellishment on a simpler stitch. Worked on back stitch, Pekinese stitch loops round each stitch and can be sewn in a similar tone or a contrasting color.

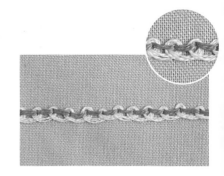

1 *Sew a row of back stitches.*

2 *Starting from the left, using the back of the needle or a tapestry needle, bring the needle out under and below the first stitch.*

3 *Take the thread up and under the third stitch, then down and under the second stitch.*

4 *Take the thread up and under the fourth stitch, then down and under the third stitch. Adjust the tension to create regular stitches, then continue along the line of back stitch.*

GARMENT/PROJECT

Use for embroidery or to decorate a garment where straight or curved lines are required, or use it as an edge or border.

FABRIC

Pekinese stitch can be worked on all fabrics.

NOTIONS AND STITCH SIZE

Use an embroidery needle to suit the weight of cloth with a large enough eye to take the embroidery floss used for the back stitch, but use the back of the needle or a blunt tapestry needle for the Pekinese stitches.

ALTERNATIVE

Use laced running stitch, chain stitch, or stem stitch for a solid line or border. Use couching as an alternative machine method with contrasting thread and cord.

PRESSING AND FINISHING

Do not flatten embroidery stitches with an iron. If necessary, iron from the wrong side on a thick, soft surface.

Laid trailing stitch

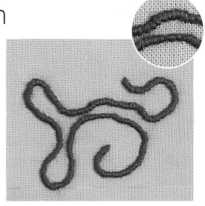

Laid trailing stitch is a form of couching (see page 98) with close stitches which conceal the thread below. The resulting stitch has depth and stands out from the cloth.

1 *Lay the thread along the sewing line and sew from right to left.*

2 *Bring the needle up at the end of the thread on the bottom edge. Take the needle over the thread and catch a small amount of fabric from below.*

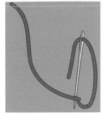

3 *Make a second stitch next to the first, concealing the thread below, and continue until the thread is completely covered.*

GARMENT/PROJECT

 Use for embroidery or to decorate a garment where a raised cord effect is required.

FABRIC

 Laid trailing stitch can be worked on all fabrics.

NOTIONS AND STITCH SIZE

 Use an embroidery needle to suit the weight of cloth with a large enough eye to take the embroidery floss used.

ALTERNATIVE

 Any linear embroidery stitch can be used to create a line, but only laid trailing stitch has such depth. A wide, short zigzag stitch sewn over a cord will give a similar effect with a sewing machine.

PRESSING AND FINISHING

 Do not flatten embroidery stitches with an iron. If necessary, iron from the wrong side on a thick, soft surface.

Florentine embroidery

Florentine embroidery is worked on single canvas. The vertical and parallel stitches build up to create a wave pattern or zigzag design across the fabric.

1 *Working from the left, bring the needle through to the surface at the start of the first stitch. Take the needle down at the end position of the stitch.*

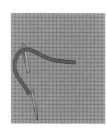

2 *Bring the needle back up near the start of the first stitch, perhaps one square higher. Take the needle down near the end of the first stitch but the same amount higher, thus creating a parallel stitch adjacent to the first.*

3 *Continue to make vertical stitches following a regular zigzag or wave pattern.*

Sewer's tip

The design can be developed as it progresses, but often a chart is followed.

GARMENT/PROJECT

Not normally used for clothing, Florentine embroidery is popular for cushions and bags.

FABRIC

This embroidery is for use on single canvas.

NOTIONS AND STITCH SIZE

Use a tapestry needle on the canvas and make stitches of an even length.

ALTERNATIVE

Florentine work is quite distinctive, but some tapestry work might provide a suitable alternative.

PRESSING AND FINISHING

Iron lightly from the wrong side if necessary.

Long and short stitch

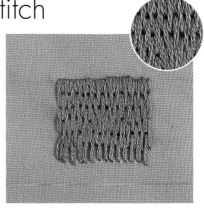

Long and short stitch is similar to satin stitch, but the stitches vary in length. It is used for larger areas where satin stitch is not suitable and a shaded effect can be produced.

1 *Start at one end of the area to be filled and bring the needle up to the surface at the top edge. Sew a straight vertical stitch, taking the needle down then bringing it back up next to the start of the first stitch.*

2 *Take the needle down parallel to the first stitch, but half the length. Take the needle down, then back up to the start of the second stitch.*

3 *Continue making these alternate long and short stitches across the work, following the line of the area to be filled. Create subsequent rows of stitches to fill the area.*

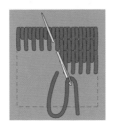

GARMENT/PROJECT

Use long and short stitch for embroidery or for decoration on a garment.

FABRIC

Long and short stitch can be worked on all fabrics.

NEEDLE AND STITCH SIZE

Use an embroidery needle to suit the weight of cloth with a large enough eye to take the embroidery floss used.

ALTERNATIVE

Use satin stitch as a filling stitch if the area is small enough. Use a short, wide zigzag stitch or freehand embroidery on a sewing machine.

PRESSING AND FINISHING

Do not flatten embroidery stitches with an iron. If necessary, iron from the wrong side on a thick, soft surface.

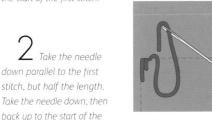

Feather stitch

Feather stitch is an embroidery stitch which—as its name suggests—has a feathery effect. It is created in a similar way to a buttonhole or chain stitch but is more open.

1 *Work from top to bottom, starting in the center. Bring the needle to the surface and take it to the right and down through the fabric. Bring it back up through the fabric below and halfway between the first two needle positions. Pass the thread below the needle and pull through, catching the thread.*

2 *To make the next stitch, take the needle down to the left and bring it back up through the fabric below and halfway between the two needle positions. Pass the thread below the needle and pull through, catching the thread as before.*

3 *Continue to create feather stitches on alternate sides for the length of the work.*

Sewer's tip

Draw parallel lines on the fabric to use as a guide to keep stitches even.

GARMENT/PROJECT

 Use feather stitch for embroidery or to decorate a garment.

FABRIC

 Feather stitch can be worked on all fabrics.

NOTIONS AND STITCH SIZE

 Use an embroidery needle to suit the weight of cloth with a large enough eye to take the embroidery floss used.

ALTERNATIVE

 Double feather stitch is created when two stitches are sewn in each direction. Use fly stitches or buttonhole stitch for a similar effect. Some sewing machines have pre-programmed decorative stitches which imitate feather stitch.

PRESSING AND FINISHING

 Do not flatten embroidery stitches with an iron. If necessary, iron from the wrong side on a thick, soft surface.

Fly stitch

 Fly stitches are embroidery stitches and can be sewn singly or in rows.

1 *Work from top to bottom. Bring the needle to the surface and take it to the right and down through the fabric. Bring it back up through the fabric below and halfway between the first two needle positions. Pass the thread below the needle and pull through, catching the thread.*

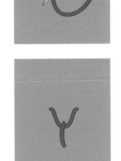

2 *Take the needle over the thread and straight down into the fabric, making a "Y" shape.*

3 *Make a second stitch in the same way directly below the first and continue, creating a row of "Y" stitches. To create single fly stitches simply finish each stitch with a tiny catch stitch holding the "V" in place.*

GARMENT/PROJECT

 Use fly stitch for embroidery or to decorate a garment.

FABRIC

 Fly stitch can be worked on all fabrics.

NOTIONS AND STITCH SIZE

 Use an embroidery needle to suit the weight of cloth with a large enough eye to take the embroidery floss used.

ALTERNATIVE

 Feather stitch or buttonhole stitch might be suitable. Some sewing machines have pre-programmed decorative stitches which imitate a row of fly stitches.

PRESSING AND FINISHING

 Do not flatten embroidery stitches with an iron. If necessary, iron from the wrong side on a thick, soft surface.

Twisted chain

Twisted chain stitch is an alternative chain stitch for lines in embroidery. It produces quick and effective straight and curved lines with a textured effect.

1 *Bring the needle through to the surface at the start of the sewing line. Then take the needle back down close to where it came up, but slightly below and to the left. Bring it back up to the surface at the end position of the first stitch. Loop the thread under the point of the needle then pull the needle through. Adjust the stitch to make a neat loop.*

2 *Take the needle back down below and to the left of the previous loop. Bring it back up at the end position of the next stitch. Loop the thread under the point of the needle then pull it through. Adjust as before.*

3 *Continue to create the appearance of a chain of twisted links and finish by catching the final loop with a small stitch to ensure the chain does not come undone.*

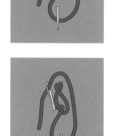

GARMENT/PROJECT

Use twisted chain stitch for embroidery or to decorate a garment.

FABRIC

Twisted chain stitch can be worked on all fabrics.

NOTIONS AND STITCH SIZE

Use an embroidery needle to suit the weight of cloth with a large enough eye to take the embroidery floss used.

ALTERNATIVE

Use ordinary chain stitch, Pekinese stitch, stem stitch, or laced running stitch for a solid outline or border.

PRESSING AND FINISHING

Do not flatten embroidery stitches with an iron. If necessary, iron from the wrong side on a thick, soft surface.

Heavy chain stitch

Heavy chain stitch is an alternative chain stitch for bolder, stronger lines in embroidery.

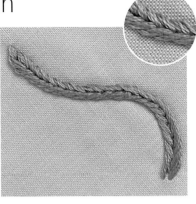

1 *Bring the needle through to the surface and make a short stitch along the sewing line at the start of the work, taking the needle through to the wrong side.*

2 *Bring the needle up one stitch further on and pass it under the first stitch without catching the fabric. Take the needle back down in the same position as it came up.*

3 *Bring the needle to the surface one stitch further along the sewing line and pass it under the first stitch as before, taking it round the last chain.*

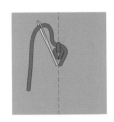

4 *Bring the needle to the surface a stitch further along and continue to create chain stitches, passing the needle under the two preceding loops each time.*

GARMENT/PROJECT

Use heavy chain stitch for bold lines in embroidery or to decorate a garment.

FABRIC

Heavy chain stitch can be worked on all fabrics.

NOTIONS AND STITCH SIZE

Use an embroidery needle to suit the weight of cloth with a large enough eye to take the embroidery floss used. Use the back of the needle when taking the thread under the loops to prevent catching the fabric.

ALTERNATIVE

Use ordinary chain stitch, Pekinese stitch, or stem stitch for a solid outline or border.

PRESSING AND FINISHING

Do not flatten embroidery stitches with an iron. If necessary, iron from the wrong side on a thick, soft surface.

French knots

French knots are individual stitches that can be used singly, clustered in a regular pattern, or scattered as a filling stitch. They can be used to add texture and are often used to depict flower centers and stamens.

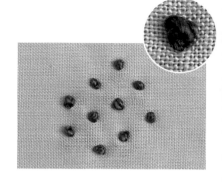

1 *Bring the needle through to the surface in the stitch position. Wrap the thread around the needle twice and insert it back into the fabric where the thread emerged.*

2 *Ease the knot onto the fabric surface, holding it with the spare thumb, and pull the needle through to the wrong side. Secure the thread end on the wrong side, or bring the needle up to the position of the next knot.*

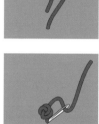

GARMENT/PROJECT

French knots are used for embroidery and can be used to decorate cushions, bags, and garments.

FABRIC

French knots can be worked on all fabrics.

NOTIONS AND STITCH SIZE

Use an embroidery needle to suit the weight of cloth with a large enough eye to take the embroidery floss used.

ALTERNATIVE

Single chain stitches (lazy daisy stitch), bullion knots, or satin stitch.

PRESSING AND FINISHING

Do not flatten embroidery stitches with an iron. If necessary, iron from the wrong side on a thick, soft surface.

Bullion knots

Larger than French knots, these are longer, individual stitches also made by twisting the thread around the needle.

1
Bring the needle up at one end of the knot and make a small back stitch, taking the needle down through the fabric at the other end.

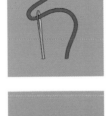

2
Bring the needle back up to the first position and wind the thread around the needle several times. Ease the needle through the wound thread, holding it with the spare thumb.

3
Take the needle back down through the fabric at the other end of the stitch, leaving the wrapped thread on the surface. Secure the thread on the wrong side.

GARMENT/PROJECT

Bullion knots are used for embroidery to add texture and are often used to depict flowers or leaves. They can be used to decorate cushions, bags, and garments.

FABRIC

Bullion knots can be worked on all fabrics.

NOTIONS AND STITCH SIZE

Use an embroidery needle to suit the weight of cloth with a large enough eye to take the embroidery floss used.

ALTERNATIVE

Single chain stitches (lazy daisy stitch), French knots, or satin stitch.

PRESSING AND FINISHING

Do not flatten embroidery stitches with an iron. If necessary, iron from the wrong side on a thick, soft surface.

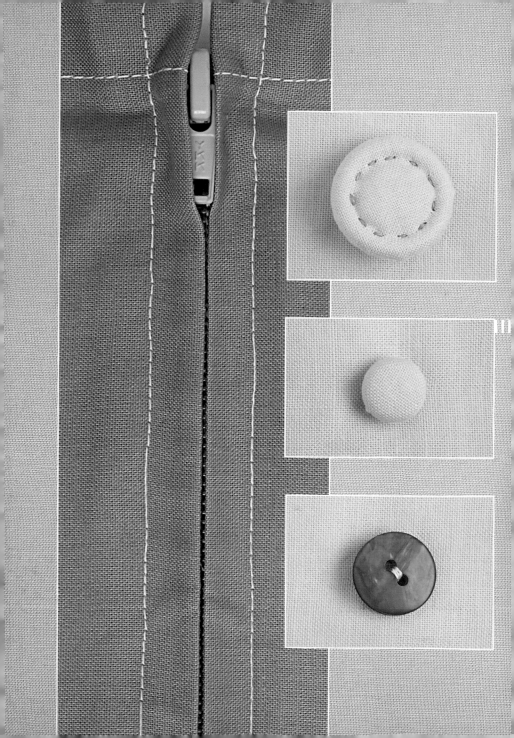

Techniques & Applications

Whether it's seams or hems, zippers or buttons, you'll want to create the best finish for your sewing projects. Look no further than these pages, which will guide you through the essentials with ease.

Seams, hems, edges, and fastenings

There are many ways to join pieces of fabric together or to finish an edge or hem, but it's important that you choose the most suitable method for your project and the fabric being used. You'll also need to select the appropriate needle and thread, so there's plenty of advice to follow if you need it. And if you want to take your seams, hems, and edges that little bit further, try experimenting with some of the additional ideas.

Plain seam

A plain seam is the easiest and most versatile method of joining two pieces of fabric together.

1
With right sides placed together, pin along the sewing line ⅝ in. (1.5cm) from the edge of the fabric.

2
Set the sewing machine to straight stitch and sew along the line, removing pins in the process.

3
Press the seam open when completed.

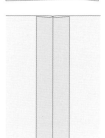

Sewer's tip

The raw edges may be neatened by serging or overcasting with a sewing machine.

GARMENT/PROJECT

Use a plain seam whenever two pieces of fabric need to be joined— either for a straight or curved seam.

FABRIC

Use for any fabrics.

NOTIONS AND STITCH SIZE

Use a size 11 needle for most tasks unless a very fine or heavy fabric is being sewn (see page 14). Stitch length will also depend on the fabric, and a stretch stitch and needle will be needed for knitted cloth.

ALTERNATIVE

Instead of pressing the seam allowances open, press them to one side and top stitch through all layers from the right side.

PRESSING AND FINISHING

Iron the stitches flat, then separate the layers and open the seam. Press the seam open from the wrong side, using the point of the iron. (Do not press the whole iron over the seam allowances.) Then turn the fabric over and lightly hover the iron over the surface of the seam. Use a pressing cloth to protect a delicate fabric.

French seam

A French seam looks like a plain seam from the right side and a tuck on the wrong side. It is a neat way to finish a straight seam if a serger is not available. It is not suitable for a curved seam.

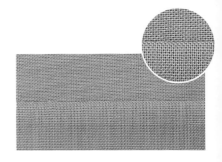

1 *With the wrong sides of the fabric together, machine ¼ in. (0.6cm) from the fabric edge with a straight stitch.*

2 *Press the seam open, then trim the raw edges to approximately ⅛ in. (0.3cm).*

3 *Fold the seam the opposite way, so that the right sides are together and the seam is pressed out to the edge. Sew a seam ¼ in. (0.6cm) from the edge, then press to finish. All the raw edges will be enclosed inside the seam.*

GARMENT/PROJECT

 French seams are often used in children's clothing, shirts, blouses, and lightweight dresses.

FABRIC

 Ideal for lightweight, sheer, and transparent fabrics as the neat finish that is produced is sometimes visible through the cloth.

NOTIONS AND STITCH SIZE

 Use a fine needle (size 9) and polyester or cotton thread, depending on the fabric chosen. A fine ball point needle can be used for stretch fabrics.

ALTERNATIVE

 A hairline seam (see page 125) or a mock French seam could be used. For a mock French seam, place the right sides together and sew ⅝ in. (1.5cm) from the edge to create a seam. Fold the raw edges to the inside and top stitch together.

PRESSING AND FINISHING

 When completed, press the French seam to one side. It doesn't matter whether this is to the center or to the side, but be consistent throughout the garment. For horizontal seams, press downward.

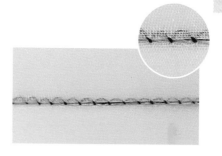

Hairline seam

A hairline seam is narrower than a French seam, and ideal for transparent fabric where a plain seam would be visible through the cloth. It does not have the strength of some other seams.

1 *Place the wrong sides of the fabric together and machine a straight line of stitching ½ in. (1.2cm) from the edge.*

2 *Machine a second row of stitching adjacent to the first one. Trim very close to the two rows of stitching.*

3 *Press the seam flat and fold round. This means the right sides are now together and the seam created is on the edge.*

4 *Using a narrow zigzag stitch approximately ¹⁄₁₆ in. (1mm) wide, machine across the edge enclosing all the raw edges inside.*

GARMENT/PROJECT

This seam is suitable for the long straight seams of a skirt or dress in a transparent fabric where there is no pressure on the seam, for example, an organza overskirt or a chiffon blouse.

FABRIC

Use on organza, chiffon, or organdie. It is useful for any fine, lightweight fabric with transparent qualities.

NOTIONS AND STITCH SIZE

A very fine new needle is essential for sewing this seam on fine fabrics. A larger or blunt needle will catch and pull threads of the cloth, damaging the appearance. Needle: size 9; stitch length: ¹⁄₁₆ in. (1mm); stitch width: ¹⁄₁₆ in. (1mm).

ALTERNATIVE

A French seam (see page 124) could be used, or a rolled hem (page 69) sewn with a serger would work well.

PRESSING AND FINISHING

The seam can be ironed flat as it is so fine. Use a pressing cloth to protect the surface of the fabric.

Flat-fell seam

A flat-fell seam has the seam allowances tucked under and sewn down with a second row of stitching. It is useful for reversible garments, sportswear, and menswear, or where added strength is required.

1 *Place the wrong sides of the fabric together and sew ⅝ in. (1.5cm) from the edge.*

2 *Press the seam allowances to one side and trim the under seam allowance to ⅛ in. (0.3cm).*

3 *Press the edge of the upper seam allowance under by ¼ in. (0.6cm). Edge stitch along the fold through all layers to finish.*

GARMENT/PROJECT

This is a strong seam suitable for jeans, sportswear, menswear, and children's clothes, for seams that come under stress or for garments that are washed frequently. It is also suitable for reversible garments as it looks good from both sides.

FABRIC

Use for most fabrics except those that are very thick.

NOTIONS AND STITCH SIZE

Choose a needle suitable for the fabric weight (see page 14). Use a straight stitch for the seams. Lengthen the stitch for thicker fabric and shorten it for very fine fabric.

ALTERNATIVE

A plain seam with the seam allowances pressed to one side with a top stitch on the surface will have a similar appearance to a flat-fell seam. A welt seam or double-welt seam could also be used.

PRESSING AND FINISHING

Use the iron to control the fabric whilst making the seam and to flatten it when completed. If necessary, use a pressing cloth to protect the surface.

Welt seam

A welt seam has a similar appearance to a flat-fell seam but is less bulky, so is suitable for heavier or thicker fabrics.

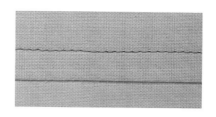

1 *With right sides together, stitch a plain seam ⅝ in. (1.5cm) from the edge.*

2 *Press the seam allowances to one side and trim the under seam allowance to ¼ in. (0.6cm).*

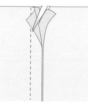

3 *Leave the upper seam allowance at ⅝ in. (1.5cm) and baste through all layers.*

4 *From the right side, top stitch through all layers ¼ in. (0.6cm) from the seam.*

GARMENT/PROJECT

Use a welt or double-welt seam for jeans and garments made in heavyweight, bulky fabrics.

FABRIC
Use on thick, bulky fabrics that do not fray badly. It is ideal for synthetic suede and leather.

NOTIONS AND STITCH SIZE
As welt seams are generally used on thicker fabrics use a large size 14 or 16 needle and lengthen the straight stitch. Use a thread that's strong and of a good quality.

ALTERNATIVE
A flat-fell seam is a good alternative. A top-stitched plain seam, with both seam allowances pressed to one side, could also be used.

PRESSING AND FINISHING
Press with an iron when completed. Use a pressing cloth to protect the surface if necessary.

Sewer's tip

A double-welt seam has a second row of edge stitching close to the seam line.

Lapped seam

Lapped seams are ideal for fabrics that don't fray, like suede and leather. They are also suitable for yokes and small areas in woven and knitted fabrics.

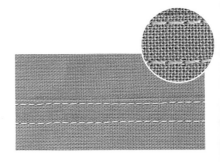

1 *For leather and suede (and non-fraying fabrics), trim away the seam allowance on the upper piece. For woven and knitted fabrics, fold along the seam line on the upper piece.*

2 *Lap the trimmed or folded edge onto the seam line of the other piece of fabric. Hold the layers together with pins, basting, or—in the case of leather— a fusible tape or glue.*

3 *Should you wish to add a second row of stitching, edge stitch the fabrics together and top stitch ¼ in. (0.6cm) away.*

GARMENT/PROJECT

Use lapped seams for leather or suede jackets or waistcoats; and on the yokes of shirts, dresses, and children's clothes.

FABRIC

Use on leather, suede, and their synthetic alternatives; and on lightweight fabrics for areas where little stress is applied to the seam.

NOTIONS AND STITCH SIZE

For leather and suede use a leather needle, a slightly longer stitch, and polyester thread. Use fabric glue rather than basting to hold the layers together for stitching. Sewing with a roller foot or a walking foot will make machining easier as these feet will not stick to the fabric. For woven and knitted fabrics use a suitable needle for the cloth weight.

ALTERNATIVE

In a lightweight fabric a plain, top-stitched seam could be used.

PRESSING AND FINISHING

For leather and suede, press with a dry iron and use brown wrapping paper as a pressing cloth. For most dress fabrics, use a stream iron and protect with a pressing cloth if necessary.

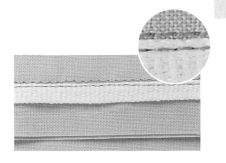

Taped seam

Sometimes seams need to be stabilized with tape to stop them from stretching. Shoulder seams, necklines, and waistlines need this when made up in knitted, loosely woven, or bias-cut fabric.

1 *Stitch the seam to be taped with a plain seam. Press the seam allowances together to one side.*

2 *Place the tape on the seam allowance that will lie furthest away from the surface of the fabric, with the edge adjacent to the seam line. Stitch the tape through the seam allowances and close to the edge next to the seam line.*

GARMENT/PROJECT

Use where seams need to be stabilized on shoulders and necklines, for example, babies' clothes and T shirts.

FABRIC

Use for shoulders in knitted, stretchy fabrics, and those cut on the bias.

NOTIONS AND STITCH SIZE

For knitted fabrics use a stretch or ball point needle in a size to suit the weight of the cloth (see page 14). Choose a narrow ¼ in. (0.6cm) cotton or polyester twill tape to stabilize seams.

ALTERNATIVE

Stitch tape into the seam in one process (as mentioned in the note above) if the tape will not be folded over and produce extra bulk.

PRESSING AND FINISHING

Press the seam and allowances flat from the wrong side, then press them to one side. Use a pressing cloth if ironing on the surface.

Sewer's tip
Although it is very common to stitch the tape at the same time as machining the seam, this often means that the tape is folded over when the seam is completed and pressed. This creates a double thickness of tape that can be bulky.

Boned seam

Boning (plastic and solid or coiled metal) can be added to seams to emphasize the figure and hold bodices so close to the body that they stay up without the need for straps. It also improves the finish by eliminating wrinkles from seams.

GARMENT/PROJECT

Use boning for bridal and evening wear where a close-fitting bodice will emphasize figure shape; it may even eliminate the need for straps. It will also remove wrinkles.

FABRIC

Boning can be carried out on all fabrics decorated with beads and embroidery. Velvet, lace (if underlined), and silk are all suitable.

NOTIONS AND STITCH SIZE

Use a needle suitable for the cloth (see page 14) and straight stitches for boning. If the fabric is fine, shorten the stitch length a little. Use ¾ in. (1.8cm) wide satin bias binding, as the boning will slide through the seam casing easily.

ALTERNATIVE

The casing can be stitched by hand with an overcasting stitch (see page 37). Some boning comes with a ready-made casing to save the need for bias tape. Others have a flange of fabric attached so this can be stitched direct to the seam allowance.

PRESSING AND FINISHING

After the bone is inserted do not iron.

1 With the right sides of the fabric together, sew a plain seam ⅝ in. (1.5cm) from the edge.

2 Press the seam open. If the seam is curved, snip the seam allowances.

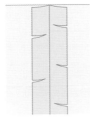

3 Working from the wrong side, place a length of ¾ in. (1.8cm) wide satin bias binding over the open seam. Center it over the seam, with the wrong side downward, and pin and baste the edge of the tape to the seam allowance below it.

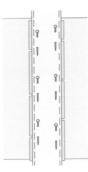

4 Stitch the binding to the seam allowance close to the folded edge. This has created a casing to house the boning.

5 Stitch across the top of the seam to close it.

6 Insert the boning into the seam casing and push it fully to the end. Mark the length required, remove the boning, and cut to length.

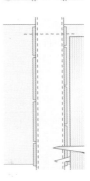

7 Reinsert the boning and stitch across the bottom of the casing to hold the boning in place.

Sewer's tip

When cutting boning, curve the ends to remove any sharp corners to prevent them from wearing through the casing and lining of the garment.

Exposed seam

As a feature, some designers deliberately sew seams inside out leaving them exposed and visible on the right side. These are sometimes serged or deliberately distressed to create a ragged effect.

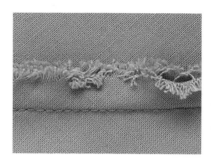

1 *With wrong sides together sew a seam ⅝ in. (1.5cm) from the edge.*

2 *Roll the fabric up like a sausage with the raw edges level. Distress the edges with a toothbrush to deliberately fray them.*

3 *Unroll the seam and press up to the distressed edges. "Finger press" the seam open.*

GARMENT/PROJECT

Jackets, skirts, and bags are all suitable for exposed seams.

FABRIC

Woolen tweed, soft denims, and loosely woven cottons are suitable. Use on bias-cut fabric for a really good finish.

NOTIONS AND STITCH SIZE

Use a needle to suit the fabric weight (see page 14) and a straight stitch.

ALTERNATIVE

Cut a bias strip of fabric the length of the seam and fold lengthwise. With right sides of the seam together, sew a plain seam enclosing the folded bias strip with the raw edges outward. Distress the bias strip on the right side. This is a good alternative when the seam is cut on the grain but a bias ragged edge is the effect wanted.

PRESSING AND FINISHING

Iron up to the ragged edge. Do not flatten the deliberately distressed finish but "finger press" to finish.

Hemming-stitched hem

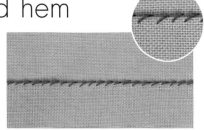

The raw edge of a hem can be neatened in a variety of ways. Some methods are more versatile than others. A double-folded hem finished with hemming stitch is a secure way to take up a hem.

1 *Mark the finished length of the hem with chalk or pins.*

2 *Fold along this edge and baste. Trim off excess fabric and level the hem to approximately 1–1½ in. (2.5–3cm).*

3 *Fold the raw edge under by ¼–½ in. (0.6–1.2cm).*

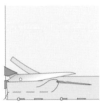

4 *Secure the thread on the left at a seam and take a small slanting stitch picking up one or two threads from the fabric. Next, catch the fold of the hem with the needle and pull through. Continue to make small, regular, slanting stitches to secure the hem.*

GARMENT/PROJECT

Use hemming to finish hems on skirts, pants, and sleeves.

FABRIC

Use on thicker fabrics where the stitches disappear into the depth of the cloth. The hemming stitches will be visible from the right side of a fine, thin fabric. Use to finish the inside of a waistband on pants or skirts.

NOTIONS AND STITCH SIZE

Use a fine needle which will not leave holes in the fabric. Use thread which is a good color match or one shade darker, as it will be less visible if it shows through to the surface. Silk thread will knot less often than cotton or polyester thread.

ALTERNATIVE

Slip stitch and lock stitch are good alternative hand-hemming methods. Use a blind hemming stitch, in conjunction with a blind hem foot, on the sewing machine.

PRESSING AND FINISHING

Press lightly from the wrong side on a well-padded ironing board to prevent a ridge showing along the hem.

Slip-stitched hem

The raw edge of a hem can be neatened in a variety of ways. Some methods are more versatile than others. A double-folded hem finished with slip stitch is almost invisible, even on very lightweight fabrics.

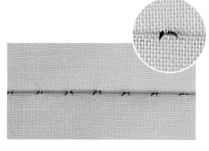

1 Mark the finished hem with chalk or pins.

2 Fold along this edge and baste. Trim off excess fabric and level the hem to approximately 1–1½ in. (2.5–3cm).

3 Fold the raw edge under by ¼–½ in. (0.6–1.2cm).

4 Secure the thread end at a seam on the right and pick up one or two threads of the fabric with the needle. Next, slip the needle through the fold of the hem and bring the needle out ¼ in. (0.6cm) away. Pick up another one or two stitches from the fabric and then again through the fold of the hem. Repeat along the length of the hem.

GARMENT/PROJECT

Use slip stitch to hem a garment made in a lightweight fabric where hemming stitch isn't suitable. Use it to attach linings or trimmings to clothes and bags.

FABRIC

Use when hemming lightweight fabrics.

NEEDLE AND STITCH SIZE

Use a small needle and small hand stitches to get a secure finish. Short lengths of silk thread will not knot or tangle.

ALTERNATIVE

Use hemming, lock stitch, or herringbone as alternative hand hem finishes, or a blind hemming stitch in conjunction with a blind hem foot if using a sewing machine.

PRESSING AND FINISHING

Press lightly from the wrong side on a well-padded ironing board to prevent a ridge showing along the hem.

Lock-stitched hem

Use this stitch for clothes and drapes. It holds when the thread breaks—as each stitch is independent the hem will not unravel fully. Only a small section of hem will need to be repaired.

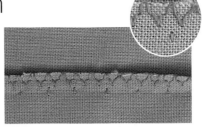

1 *Fold up the hem and neaten the raw edge if necessary.*

2 *Fold back the neatened edge by about ⅛ in (0.3cm) and secure the thread in the hem. Pick up one or two threads of the fabric on the stitching line and some threads on the hem adjacent to this.*

3 *Pull the thread until almost through, then take the needle through the loop created by the thread. Pull gently to complete the stitch. Make further stitches approximately ½ in. (1.2cm) apart (see page 36).*

GARMENT/PROJECT

Use lock stitch for all garment and drape hems requiring an invisible finish.

FABRIC

Works well on all fabrics, but especially useful on those with a stretch.

NEEDLE AND STITCH SIZE

Use a fine needle which will not leave holes in the fabric. Keep stitches long and regular so that they will not be seen from the right side. Use silk thread to reduce tangling and knotting.

ALTERNATIVE

Like lock stitch, a herringbone stitch will allow a fabric to stretch. Some sewing machines have a blind hem stitch suitable for stretch fabrics.

PRESSING AND FINISHING

As with all hems, press lightly to prevent a ridge becoming visible along the hem.

Sewer's tip

For a double-folded hem catch through both layers.

Hong Kong finish

A Hong Kong finish is an ideal way to neaten hems and seams. Bias cut strips in habotai silk or lining wrap round the raw edges to prevent them from fraying and give a neat, bulk-free finish. Use it as a decorative finish on pockets too.

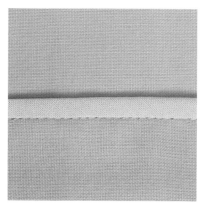

On a hem

To neaten a raw edge

GARMENT/PROJECT

Use a Hong Kong finish to neaten raw edges on hems of skirts, pants, and jackets, and for a tidy finish on seams of unlined jackets, skirts, and pants. Also use it as a decorative edge round pocket flaps.

FABRIC

Use on medium to heavyweight fabrics like crêpes, wools, and tweeds. Use fine silk or lining for the bias-cut strips.

NOTIONS AND STITCH SIZE

Use a size 12 needle and a straight stitch of 12 stitches to 1 in. (2.5mm). A rotary cutter (with a self-healing mat) is useful for cutting the 1¼ in. (3.2cm) strips, but long-bladed sharp scissors will do.

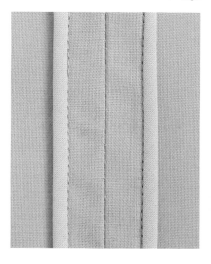

ALTERNATIVE

Edges bound with a bias binding will have a similar appearance to a Hong Kong finish but will be more bulky. "Seams Great" is a product which will neaten edges. Pull the tape slightly and it curls over the raw edge. Machine this in place with a straight stitch or small zigzag stitch.

PRESSING AND FINISHING

Iron through all stages of making for a good result. Take care when pressing the finished seams to prevent a ridge from forming on the surface of the garment.

1 *Cut bias strips of fine silk or lining 1¼ in. (3.2cm) wide to match or contrast with the garment being neatened.*

2 *Place the bias strip right side down on top of the seam or hem with the raw edges level. Pin, then stitch in place ¼ in (0.6cm) from the edge.*

3 *Trim to ⅛ in. (0.3cm) and fold the bias strip round the raw edge and under the seam allowance.*

4 *Pin in the ditch where the strip meets the fabric to hold the strip in place. Keep all layers out of the way and stitch in the ditch for the length of the seam or hem edge.*

5 *Trim away any excess and press flat. As the strip is cut on the bias it can be trimmed close to the stitching—it will not fray.*

Sewer's tip

For a seam finish use a standard plain seam ⅝–1 in. (1.5–2.5cm) wide, and press it open. For a hem, neaten the edge with the Hong Kong finish before folding it up and securing with a lock stitch.

Faced or false hem

Where a deep hem has to be made on a wide or flared skirt, excess fabric results on the inside that needs to be gathered up. A far better method is to use a faced or false hem; the excess hem is cut off and a separate hem is cut in the same shape, then sewn in place. This forms a flat smooth hem with no unnecessary bulk.

GARMENT/PROJECT

Use a false or faced hem on full, shaped skirts, or those with a train.

FABRIC

Use on all weights of fabric.

NOTIONS AND STITCH SIZE

Use a machine needle to suit the fabric being sewn (see page 14) and a fine short needle for hand stitching. Use a silk thread when hand sewing to reduce tangling and knotting. A 6 in. (15cm) ruler is a handy tool for marking a faced or false hem.

ALTERNATIVE

A narrow hem will be less bulky than a deep hem on a full-shaped skirt, but a deep hem achieves an added weight which helps a skirt to drape well.

PRESSING AND FINISHING

Iron through all stages of making, but take care when pressing the finished hem as ridges from the seam at the hem line and the top folded edge may show through. Iron lightly and use a pressing cloth to protect the surface of the fabric.

1 *Establish the required level of the hem and add ⅝ in. (1.5cm). Cut off the excess below this.*

2 *Cut facings, the same shape as the hem, for each panel of the skirt (including seam allowances). For a short skirt this should be approximately 2 in. (5cm) wide, and for a wedding dress or evening skirt approximately 3½ in. (9cm) wide.*

3 *Place each panel onto the skirt with right sides facing and the lower edges level. Fold the seam allowances of the hem facing under to match the seams. Pin and machine each panel in place ⅝ in. (1.5cm) from the lower edge. Layer the raw edges to reduce bulk and under stitch (sedge stitch) through the hem and raw edges.*

4 *Press the panels up to the inside with the seam at hem level just to the inside of the skirt. Match up the folded seam allowances at each seam and stitch together with a ladder stitch (see page 35).*

5 *Snip and turn the top edge of the hem under, and sew to the body of the skirt with a lock stitch or slip stitch.*

Interfaced hem

For a soft tailored hem a bias strip of interfacing is added within the fold of the hem. A fusible interfacing can be used, but silk organza creates an excellent finish.

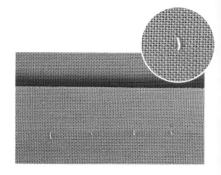

1 *Mark the finished hem level with a basting thread and cut a bias strip of silk organza with ¼ in. (0.6cm) added. Press a fold in the strip ⅝ in. (1.5cm) from one edge.*

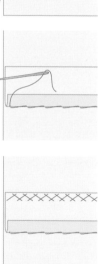

2 *Place the fold on to the basted hem line with the strip extending into the garment and not the hem. Sew the organza strip to the hem line with long catch stitches that catch the main fabric but do not show through to the right side.*

3 *With a herringbone stitch (see page 40) lightly catch the top edge of the organza to the fabric, making sure the stitches do not show on the right side.*

4 *Sew the hem to the organza strip with a lock stitch.*

GARMENT/PROJECT

Suitable for couture garments and the hems of sleeves and jackets which will be lined.

FABRIC

Use on silk and wool tweeds and fine worsted wools and crêpes. Although a fusible woven interfacing can be used silk organza cut into bias strips gives a good result.

NOTIONS AND STITCH SIZE

Hand stitch with a fine short needle and silk thread as this will not tangle or knot. Cut the bias strips with a rotary cutter or with long-bladed shears.

ALTERNATIVE

Use a woven, fusible interfacing and cut into bias strips. Position the strip on the edge of the hem, extending ⅝ in. (1.5cm) over the fold of the hem into the garment. Lock stitch the hem to the fused interlining to hold it in place.

PRESSING AND FINISHING

Iron lightly, using a pressing cloth to protect the surface of the fabric.

Horsehair braid

A hem finished with a lightweight nylon "horsehair braid" has a stiffened effect ideal for mid-length and long evening skirts. Wide and narrow braid can be used and top stitched or hand stitched in place. It forms a stiff, crisp finish on evening and bridal wear.

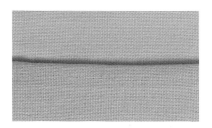

1 Mark the length of the finished hem, then add the width of the braid and ¼ in. (0.6cm) below this line. Trim at this level.

2 Place the horsehair braid over the edge of the hem ¼ in. (0.6cm) from the edge on the wrong side of the skirt. Stitch with a straight stitch close to the edge through the braid and hem.

3 Fold the braid to the inside and fold up once more to conceal the braid. Top stitch (and edge stitch too if desired) narrow horsehair braid in place, sewing from the right side of the skirt. For wider horsehair braid top stitch or hand stitch in place with slip stitch or lock stitch.

GARMENT/PROJECT

The full skirts of bridal gowns and evening skirts benefit from a crisp edge made with horsehair braid.

FABRIC

Use on duchesse satin, silk brocade, velvet, and other special occasion fabrics

NOTIONS AND STITCH SIZE

Use a size 11 needle unless the fabric is particularly thick or heavy, in which case a size 14 will be required.

ALTERNATIVE

The horsehair braid does not need to be concealed and need only be folded once; however, the coarse nylon can snag on pantyhose or undergarments. For a shaped hem, a faced hem could be used (see page 138).

PRESSING AND FINISHING

Iron the very lower edge only and use a pressing cloth to protect the surface of the fabric. A dry iron may be best for silks, which may water-mark.

Twin-needle hem

Knitted fabrics stretch when pulled, so their hems need to be stretchy too. Using a twin needle gives garments a manufactured finish on the surface and the bobbin thread, which zigzags between the two rows of stitching on the underside, provides some movement. This is ideal for hemming cotton knits like T-shirts.

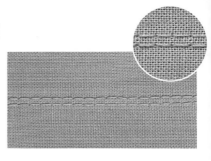

1 *Finish the raw edge with a zigzag, overcast, or serger stitch.*

2 *Fold up the hem to the required length and hold in place with pins, on the right side of the fabric.*

3 *Fit a twin needle to the machine and, following the manual instructions, thread up with two reels of thread. Drop the bobbin in place with matching thread.*

4 *With the right side of the fabric uppermost, feed the hem through the machine, stitching it in place.*

GARMENT/PROJECT

Use on stretch knits like T-shirts, sweatshirts, and fleeces.

FABRIC

Use on cotton knitted fabric and those with some stretch. Very stretchy fabrics with Lycra need to be hemmed with a serger or cover stitch machine that provide greater stretch.

NOTIONS AND STITCH SIZE

For best results use a stretch twin needle in a size 11 or 14. The width between the needles varies, but a wider space is better for hemming. Use polyester thread as it has more give than cotton thread. A walking foot also helps when sewing a twin-needle hem on stretch fabrics as the finished hem will be flat. A normal foot may cause the hem to ripple.

ALTERNATIVE

Use a pre-programmed stretch stitch, or a quilting straight stitch and a single needle but sew two parallel rows of stitching.

PRESSING AND FINISHING

Press from the hem edge in to the garment. Ironing along the edge of the hem may cause it to stretch.

Wing needle and blanket stitch hem

Decorative hems created with a wing needle are ideal for table and bed linen. The broad, winged needle leaves a hole where each stitch is made, giving a similar effect to pulled thread work which is carried out by hand. Use a wing needle with a pre-programmed blanket stitch for best results.

1 *For greatest effect select a blanket stitch on a long, wide setting and fit the wing needle in place.*

2 *Fold up the hem and press using spray starch. This will help to stabilize the fabric.*

3 *Place the folded hem under the presser foot, ensuring that the main stitches are formed in the single layer, catching only the hem when the needle swings to the side.*

GARMENT/PROJECT

Use this hem finish for cloths, runners, and napkins for the table, or for sheets and pillowcases to add an antique finish. Use it on cotton blouses and children's dresses.

FABRIC

Use to hem natural fabrics for best results; 100 percent cotton lawn, sheeting, linen, or silk organza are all suitable. Fabrics made with synthetic fibers have an element of stretch which prevents the holes made by the needle from staying open.

NOTIONS AND STITCH SIZE

Use a wing needle with cotton thread as this is stable. Polyester thread will not hold the holes open so well as it has an element of stretch. Use spray starch to stabilize the fabric before stitching, or use a tear-away stabilizer.

ALTERNATIVE

Try a hand-stitched hem using pulled thread work (see pages 77–81) for a traditional alternative.

PRESSING AND FINISHING

Iron lightly.

Glued hem

When fabric is difficult to sew a hem can be glued or fused in place with either a fabric glue or a heat-setting film of glue. This is ideal for thick leathers, vinyl, or plastic waterproof fabrics where needle holes would either perforate or tear the plastic or damage the waterproof quality.

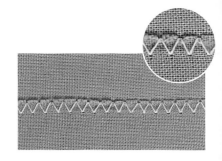

1 *Fold up a 1–2 in. (2.5–5cm) hem. If using leather or a bonded non-fraying fabric, trim to a neat finish. For woven fabrics neaten the edge.*

2 *Use fabric glue on leather and vinyl where it will not seep through to the right side, as it may discolor through time. Hold the hem with weights until it has stuck firmly. An edge stitch could be added on some leather hems as a design feature.*

3 *Alternatively use a strip of heat-fusing glue, which often comes on a paper backing, for woven fabrics. Iron the glue side onto the inside of the hem, then peel away the paper backing. Fold up the hem and iron in place.*

GARMENT/PROJECT

Use a glued hem for leather jackets, coats, and bags, which will often be lined, and for waterproof vinyl garments. Occasionally, pant and jacket hems can be finished with an iron-on fusible strip.

FABRIC

Leather, suede, vinyl, and other waterproof fabrics are suitable. Do not use a glued hem on knitted fabrics as they will not stretch.

NOTIONS AND STITCH SIZE

Use a rubber cement or PVA fabric glue for leather, suede, and vinyl. If edge stitching a glued leather hem, use a leather point needle. Use an iron-on fusible web with a peel-off backing for woven fabrics.

ALTERNATIVE

Use top stitching to hem leather, rather than glue.

PRESSING AND FINISHING

Do not iron leather or vinyl. Use a pressing cloth and steam whilst fusing the hem in place on woven fabrics.

Machine blind hem

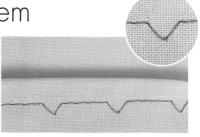

With a blind stitch foot and a pre-programmed stitch in the sewing machine, neat—almost invisible—hems can be produced on drapes and garments. The foot helps to guide the fabric into the best position for stitching, making it an easy task.

1 *Fold up the hem with a double fold.*

2 *Fold the hem back on itself leaving ¼ in. (0.6cm) of the hem showing, and pin or baste to hold in place for machining.*

3 *Set the sewing machine to a suitable blind hem stitch and attach the blind hem foot.*

4 *Use the foot as a guide and feed the folded hem through the machine to allow it to stitch in the correct position leaving tiny, almost invisible, stitches on the surface of the finished hem.*

GARMENT/PROJECT

Use a blind hem for drapes. Some skirts and pants may be hemmed with this method.

FABRIC

Use on medium to thick fabrics. On fine fabrics, the stitches will be seen on the right side.

NOTIONS AND STITCH SIZE

Use a needle suitable for the weight of fabric (see page 14), and choose a suitable blind hem stitch from the options available. Some use zigzag stitches to allow for stretch, and others use straight stitches for woven, stable fabrics. Lengthen the stitch if necessary to make the stitches on the hem further apart and so less visible on the right side.

ALTERNATIVE

A lock stitch hem is a good hand-sewn alternative.

PRESSING AND FINISHING

Press the finished hem from the wrong side along the bottom edge and under the "lip" left at the top of the hem. This ensures that no ridges will show on the right side.

Rolled hem

A rolled hem is a fine edge finish for a lightweight or sheer fabric. Traditionally rolled and hemmed by hand, the rolled hem foot attachment for the sewing machine now enables a neater hem.

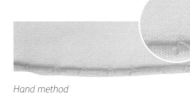

Hand method

Machine method

1 *With a straight stitch, machine ⅛ in. (0.3cm) from the raw edge. Trim close to the line of stitching.*

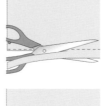

Hand method

2 *Roll the edge over with the thumb and first finger. Hem with small slip stitches.*

Machine method

2 *Attach the rolled hem foot and select straight stitch. Roll the first 1 in. (2.5cm) of the hem and sew under the presser foot.*

3 *Feed the rolled hem through the foot in front of the needle and continue to sew.*

GARMENT/PROJECT

Use a rolled hem for scarves, blouses, and skirt hems made in sheer or lightweight fabrics, and for ruffles, lingerie, and baby clothes.

FABRIC

Use on fine silks, cottons, and lightweight polyester fabrics. It is especially good for sheer fabrics.

NOTIONS AND STITCH SIZE

Use a fine short needle and silk thread when sewing hand-rolled hems. Use a size 9 or 11 needle and attach a rolled hem foot for a machined-rolled hem.

ALTERNATIVE

Use a zigzag stitch rather than a straight stitch when making a machine-rolled hem for a picot-edge effect, or use a serger rolled hem for a fine finish.

PRESSING AND FINISHING

Press flat when the hem is completed. If the edge curls this can sometimes be solved by using spray starch, but check this on a scrap of fabric first.

Fishing-line hem

This is most commonly used in conjunction with a serged rolled hem (see page 69), where the stitches are made over fishing line and the edge is fluted to make a wavy, flowing edge. It gives a firmness to ruffles in lightweight fabrics and is often seen on ballroom and evening dresses.

1 *Set the serger for rolled hemming.*

2 *Feed fishing line, with a minimum breaking strain of 18 lb. (8.2kg), under the needle and serge at least 1 in. (2.5cm) of stitches over it to secure the end.*

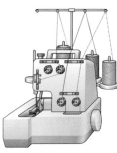

3 *Place the edge of the fabric under the fishing line and serge over the line and fabric edge, feeding them carefully through under the needle and presser foot.*

4 *When completed, manipulate the stitched edge over the fishing line, feeding it along through the stitches to create a stiff wavy edge.*

GARMENT/PROJECT

Use a fishing-line edge on the flowing skirts of evening and dance wear.

FABRIC

Use on sheer lightweight fabric where the fishing line will add a firm edge and give body to ruffles and flounces.

NOTIONS AND STITCH SIZE

Use a size 9 or 11 machine needle in the serger and matching thread in the lower looper and needle. For the upper looper, select the same thread or use a decorative thread, for example, metallic, wooly nylon, or machine embroidery floss. This will add detail to the edge. Use a short stitch length to give good coverage to the hem.

ALTERNATIVE

A lettuce edge is an attractive fluted finish to a hem, but it does not have the body of the fishing line hem. Sew fishing line into the hem when using a rolled hem foot attachment on the sewing machine.

PRESSING AND FINISHING

Press the edge before sewing in the fishing line. There is no need to iron it after this is in place.

Joining lace

When joining panels of lace a plain seam might not do the fabric justice. For best results, retaining the patterns within the lace, the panels are overlapped, stitched together, and the excess cloth cut away later.

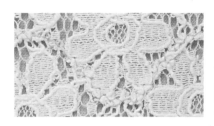

1 *Lay the seams or panels to be joined on top of one another with right sides uppermost. Pin them together.*

2 *Look carefully at the pattern and follow a dominant section of the design along the seam line with a basting stitch.*

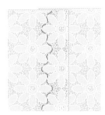

3 *Set the sewing machine to a zigzag stitch with a good matching color thread and stitch along the pattern line. This is likely to wave from side to side and will not be straight.*

4 *With small sharp scissors, trim away the raw edges close to the zigzag stitching on the right and wrong sides.*

GARMENT/PROJECT

 Use this method for bodices, skirts, and hems on wedding dresses, and evening gowns or christening gowns and children's dresses. This type of construction cannot be used where there will be stress on a seam.

FABRIC

 Join laces of all types including cotton, silk, and stretch. Use it for joining panels cut from all-over lace as well as edging laces. Use this method to attach lace to a non-lace fabric, for example, for a lace edge on the hem of a waist slip or underskirt made from an interlock polyester fabric.

NOTIONS AND STITCH SIZE

 Use a zigzag stitch of approximately ⅛ in. (3mm) wide and long, but make a sample first to check the appropriate stitch.

ALTERNATIVE

 Use a hairline seam as an alternative.

PRESSING AND FINISHING

 Iron lightly, protecting the surface of the lace.

Facings

A facing is a neat, flat way to finish the edge of a neckline or center front. It encloses all seam allowances and can strengthen an edge to take buttonholes and buttons or other fastenings. It is a neat way to finish a curved or shaped edge.

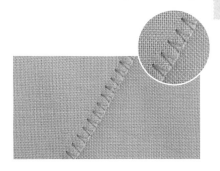

1 *Cut the facing to match the shape of the edge to be finished. Neaten the outer edge of the facing with a serger or sewing machine.*

2 *Place the right side of the facing to the right side of the garment edge and pin together. Baste if necessary.*

3 *Use a straight stitch and machine the facing to the garment edge on the sewing line. Trim and layer the seam allowance on the inside to reduce bulk.*

4 *Press the stitches flat and turn through. Press again to flatten the edge.*

GARMENT/PROJECT

Use facings to neaten edges on necklines, armholes, and jacket fronts. Use it to create a "letter box" opening to insert a zipper.

FABRIC

Use for all weights of woven and knitted fabric. However, if stretch is required it is not an appropriate method for a knitted fabric. On heavy or bulky fabrics a finer fabric can be used as a facing, for example faux fur.

NOTIONS AND STITCH SIZE

Use fusible interfacing to stabilize facings before attaching them. Use a medium length straight stitch to sew the facing in position.

ALTERNATIVE

Use a bias-bound edge or a Hong Kong finish instead of a facing. For a decorative finish attach the facing to the wrong side and press it over onto the surface of the garment.

PRESSING AND FINISHING

Press the facing to the wrong side with the seam slightly to the inside. Catch the edge with a few hand stitches at the seams to secure.

Attaching elastic

Traditionally, elastic was inserted into a casing in a garment. Manufacturers, however, now favor elastic being stitched directly in place, whether in boys' pants, girls' skirts, or in lingerie including bras, waist slips, and knickers. It is sewn onto the folded edge using a method called "quarter pinning," giving a smooth, non-bulky finish.

Elastic casing

"Quarter pin" method

GARMENT/PROJECT

Use a casing for waistbands on skirts, and for waistbands on children's pants and skirts. Use quarter pinning for sewing bras, knickers, swimwear, and skirts that are made in lightweight materials.

FABRIC

Use a casing and elastic for light- and medium-weight fabrics. Use quarter pinning for lightweight silks, satins, and knitted and woven cottons and polyesters, as well as Lycra.

NOTIONS AND STITCH SIZE

Use a stretch or ball point needle and a medium- to long-length three-step zigzag stitch. The stitch needs to be lengthened as the stitches are made with the elastic stretched so that when the elastic is relaxed the stitches shorten. Try it out on a sample first.

ALTERNATIVE

Use either a casing or quarter pinning to attach elastic. Use this method with a small normal zigzag if preferred.

PRESSING AND FINISHING

Iron up to but not over the elastic edge.

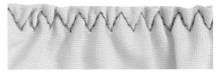

Elastic inserted into a casing

1 Fold the edge of the fabric under ⅜ in. (1cm) and fold it again by the same amount. Pin in place and baste if necessary then stitch close to the folded edge.

2 Unpick a few of the stitches in the seam on the wrong side within the casing, then feed the elastic through with a bodkin or safety pin. Cut the elastic, overlap the edges, and stitch together securely.

3 Use a slip stitch or ladder stitch to close the hole in the seam (see pages 34 and 35).

Sewing edging elastic using the "quarter pin" method

1 Measure and mark the elastic into quarters and do the same with the fabric.

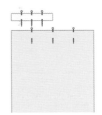

2 Match up the quarter positions and pin the elastic and fabric together, with the wrong side of the elastic to the right side of the fabric.

3 Set the machine to a three-step zigzag stitch (see page 54) and sew the elastic to the fabric, pulling the elastic while sewing. Sew each quarter at a time.

4 Fold the elastic edge to the inside. Stitch a second row of three-step zigzag with the elastic folded to the inside by pulling the elastic as before.

Bias-bound edge

Edges can be bound with bias binding to finish and to strengthen raw edges. The bound edges can finish a seam and be hidden on the inside of a garment, or they can be visible on a jacket edge, pocket flap, or collar. They can match the garment or be made with a contrasting colored fabric, and as they are bias cut they shape easily round curves and corners.

GARMENT/PROJECT

Bias binding neatens seam edges and finishes pocket flaps, collars, jacket edges, and armholes. Use bias binding to finish blanket edges, tablecloths, and napkins, as well as bags.

FABRIC

Use light- to mediumweight woven fabrics which are fairly stiff or crisp, including synthetic suede and leather-like fabrics. Stiffen softer fabrics with spray starch to make them easier to handle. Bind the edges of any fabrics to neaten them.

NOTIONS AND STITCH SIZE

Use a rotary cutter, self-healing mat, and ruler to cut accurate bias strips for best results. Use cotton or polyester thread and a needle to suit the weight of the cloth (see page 14). Use a Teflon foot or walking foot if working with leather or suede-type fabrics.

ALTERNATIVE

For neatening and binding seams on the inside of garments use "Seams Great" as an alternative. Machine this over the raw edge with a straight stitch or small zigzag stitch. Use a Hong Kong finish (see pages 136–137) as a binding alternative. It looks the same but is less bulky.

PRESSING AND FINISHING

Iron flat and protect the surface with a pressing cloth.

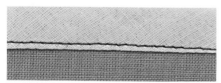

Methods of binding an edge

MAKING BIAS STRIPS FOR BINDING

Pre-made bias binding is available for edging seams but it can be made from woven fabric in the width required for a particular task. Soft fabrics are difficult to handle as bindings so choose crisp fabrics or use spray starch to stiffen softer ones.

ATTACHING BIAS EDGING

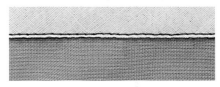

Method 1

1 Fold the fabric, bringing the cut end of the roll to meet the selvage edge (the fold is the true bias). Mark this line and from it cut parallel lines to the width required.

2 If possible, use a long enough strip to cover an edge but it may be necessary to join them with seams. Overlap the diagonal ends of the strips with the right sides together and stitch to join.

3 Fold the bias strip in half lengthwise with the wrong sides together then fold each edge into the center. Gadgets are available to help with folding.

1 Place one of the raw edges next to the edge of the fabric on the inside with the right side of the binding facing the wrong side of the fabric. Pin along the fold of the binding and stitch.

2 Fold the binding up and over the fabric edge. Tuck the seam allowance under and pin in place.

3 From the right side, top stitch the bias tape in place along the edge.

4 Where two ends of binding meet, fold over one edge and hand stitch in place to join them.

Method 2

1 *Open out the binding and place one of the raw edges next to the edge of the fabric on the outside so that the right side of the binding faces the right side of the fabric. Pin along the fold of the binding and baste if preferred. Stitch along this line with a straight stitch.*

2 *Fold the binding up and over the fabric edge. Tuck the seam allowance of the binding under and pin in place, then baste if preferred.*

3 *Stitch in the ditch between the tape and the fabric on the right side, catching the binding on the inside. Alternatively, you can hem the inner edge by hand with a hemming stitch.*

Method 3

1 *Fold the bias binding over the edge of the fabric, pinning or basting it in place.*

2 *Top stitch along the edge of the binding. Work from the right side, stitching through all layers in one step.*

Method 4

1 *Set the sewing machine to straight stitch and fit a bias binder attachment.*

2 *Feed the folded bias binding through the attachment. The needle will automatically stitch through all layers at the edge of the binding.*

Piped edge

Piping gives an attractive finish to a seam or edge. It is a strip of fabric wrapped round a cord and sandwiched between two layers of cloth.

Inserting piping

Joining piping

Double piping

GARMENT/PROJECT

Use piping for cushions, drape tie-backs, and bedding. For garments, use it on pocket flaps, to enhance seams, to define panels of an evening bodice, and on cuffs and collars. Use matching or contrasting colors and textures.

FABRIC

Use bias-cut woven fabrics or knitted strips for piping and interline with a fine cotton fabric for best results. Shiny satin piping makes an attractive contrast on silk or wool tweed garments, and contrasting colors of jersey cotton define seams on T-shirts and sweatshirts.

NOTIONS AND STITCH SIZE

Use a piping foot or zipper foot attachment to enable stitching very close to the edge of the piping. Use a needle to suit the weight and type of cloth (see page 14) and a medium-length straight stitch.

ALTERNATIVE

Edges can be finished with binding or a Hong Kong finish (see pages 136–137). A decorative braid or cord with a flange can be inserted into seams and edges.

PRESSING AND FINISHING

Iron the seam or edge flat, but protect the surface of the fabric with a pressing cloth if necessary.

Preparing piping

1 *Cut bias strips of fabric measuring the circumference of the cord plus 1¼ in. (3.2cm). This will cover the cord and provide seam allowances of ⅝ in. (1.5cm). Cut strips the same size in cotton lawn for interlining.*

2 *If possible use a long enough strip to cover the piping cord, but it may be necessary to join them with seams. Overlap the diagonal ends of the strips with the right sides together and stitch to join.*

3 *Wrap the interlining strip round the cord and baste in place.*

4 *Wrap the fabric strip over the interlining and baste this on top.*

Inserting piping to a seam or edge

1 *Place the raw edges of the piping to the right side of the fabric with the raw edges level. Pin and baste together.*

2 *Attach a piping foot to the sewing machine and stitch close to the piping.*

3 *Place the second layer of fabric to the piped fabric with right sides facing and the raw edges matching. Pin and baste through all layers.*

4 *Work from the previously piped side—use the stitching as a guide. Stitch through all layers.*

5 *Trim away any excess bulk on the inside if necessary, and layer the seam.*

Sewer's tip

The interlining layer is not always necessary.

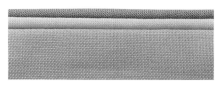

Joining piping

1 *When joining the ends of piping pull back the covering strips and cut the pieces of piping cord to butt up to each other.*

2 *Place one side of the covering strips over the cord and fold the other edge under.*

3 *Wrap this end round the other end and stitch as normal.*

Sewer's tip

To cut the fabric on the bias fold it diagonally, bringing the accurately cut end of the roll to meet the selvage edge; the fold will be on the true bias. Mark this line and from it mark parallel lines of the width required. Cut these strips accurately with long-bladed scissors or a rotary cutter.

Double piping as an edging

1 *Place the raw edges of the first piping to the right side of the fabric with the raw edges level. Pin and baste the layers together.*

2 *Place the second piece of fabric on top without the piping. Pin and baste through all layers.*

3 *Attach a piping foot to the sewing machine. Stitch close to the piping.*

4 *Add the piping cord and fold the second strip over it. Pin, baste, and machine in position, keeping close to the cord.*

5 *Attach the second layer of fabric to sandwich the piping in place, creating a double-piped edge.*

Attaching a band

Necklines, cuffs, and hems can be finished with a simple band. Use this method on garments made from woven or knitted fabrics. For sweatshirts and sportswear, ribbing can be purchased in matching and contrasting colors, although bands can be cut from the same fabric to finish edges.

Woven fabric

Knitted fabric

GARMENT/PROJECT

Attach bands to necklines, cuffs, and hems of sweatshirts and T-shirts. Use bands in woven fabrics on cuffs, hems, and front bands on wrap-over garments.

FABRIC

This is an excellent method for finishing fabrics with a knitted construction (especially if sewn with a serger), such as knitted cotton/cotton polyester mixes, fleece fabrics, and sports fabric containing Lycra. It can be used for stitching woven fabrics, but this is less common.

NOTIONS AND STITCH SIZE

For knitted fabrics use a stretch needle or ball point needle with polyester thread. If using a sewing machine choose a stretch stitch and attach a walking foot for best results.

ALTERNATIVE

Use facings to finish necklines and center front edges. Add piping to the seam on woven bands for a decorative edge.

PRESSING AND FINISHING

Press the neatened seam allowances flat against the inside of the garment.

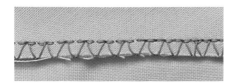

Woven fabric

1 Cut a straight grain or bias strip of fabric to the length required. It should be twice the width with seam allowances added.

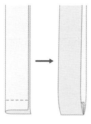

2 Fold the ends with right sides together and stitch across. Trim and turn through to form the lower hem edges.

3 Fold the bands in half lengthways with the wrong sides together. Place the band to the right side of the fabric, with the raw edges level and pin through all layers.

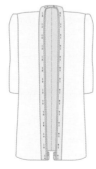

4 Stitch the band in position with a serger or use a sewing machine and neaten the raw edges with a zigzag or overcast stitch.

Knitted fabric

1 Measure the length of the edge to which the band is to be sewn.

2 Cut a length of ribbing or a strip of fabric shorter than the edge it is to be attached to. It should be twice the width with seam allowances added. Sew the short ends to form a circle.

3 Place the folded strip (right side outward) against the right side of the garment edge, matching up the raw edges, and quarter pin (see page 151).

4 Pin and sew through all the layers with a serger, or a sewing machine with the walking foot attached.

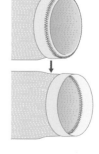

Top and edge stitching

These are rows of decorative stitching visible on the surface of fabric to define the structure of a garment and to reinforce areas. Top stitching is close to the edge of seams; edge stitching is sewn right on the edge to emphasize it and create a crisper finish. Use top stitching and edge stitching together or individually.

1 *Use either top stitch thread, buttonhole twist, or a double thread with a top stitch needle. Prepare the machine and set it to a slightly longer stitch.*

2 *For top stitching, sew a regular distance ⅛ to ⅜ in. (0.3 to 1cm) away from the edge of the fabric. An edge stitching foot can be bought to guide the needle along the edge of the garment.*

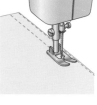

3 *Leave tails of thread at the end of the work. These can be threaded and taken through to the wrong side to secure them.*

GARMENT/PROJECT

Use top and/or edge stitching to define seams on jeans and casual skirts. Use them to decorate collar edges, cuffs, and hems, and to strengthen patch pockets. Use edge stitching on its own to sharpen a soft edge on camisoles and nightdresses.

FABRIC

Suitable for use on all fabrics.

NOTIONS AND STITCH SIZE

Lengthen the stitch and choose top stitching thread or buttonhole twist for more visible stitching. Use double thread if top stitching thread isn't available. Use a size 16 top stitch needle to sew through the extra layers and hold the thicker thread without shredding. Use a similar or contrasting color for top and edge stitching.

ALTERNATIVE

Use a twin needle for two parallel top stitching lines or select a decorative stitch. Hand prick stitch is used on a collar edge for a jacket or coat.

PRESSING AND FINISHING

Press to flatten the stitched seam or edge. Protect the surface with a pressing cloth if necessary.

Ditch stitching

Stitching in the ditch is a useful technique to sew down an edge from the right side in the well or ditch so that the stitches are almost hidden. It is used for bindings and waistbands where traditionally a hand-hemming stitch would have been used on the wrong side of the garment.

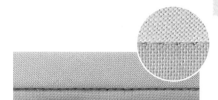

1 *Prepare the binding or waistband as normal, taking all the raw edges to the wrong side.*

2 *From the right side, pin in the ditch and through all the layers below.*

3 *Attach a zipper foot to the sewing machine and set for straight stitch.*

4 *Pull the binding or waistband gently to the right, revealing the ditch, and turn the handle to lower the needle into the ditch. Stitch along the ditch, keeping the band out of the way.*

GARMENT/PROJECT

Use this technique for waistbands on skirts and pants and bound edges on sleeveless tops, necklines, and jackets.

FABRIC

Use on all types of fabric from light to heavy, and thin to thick. It can also be used on stretchy fabrics.

NOTIONS AND STITCH SIZE

Use a size 14 needle and a good color matching thread.

ALTERNATIVE

Fold the raw edges to conceal them on the wrong side and finish with hand hemming.

PRESSING AND FINISHING

Use the iron to encourage the binding to fall back over the ditch to hide the stitches.

Appliqué

Appliqué is a decorative technique where a design is added to the surface of a fabric and stitched in place by hand or machine. Traditionally this was a slow process, but new products allow quick and easy results by fusing the design onto the fabric rather than basting them in place.

GARMENT/PROJECT

Use appliqué to decorate cushions, bags, beanbags, and garments where a bold design is required.

FABRIC

Light- and mediumweight woven fabrics are suitable, and those made from natural fibers are easiest to handle. Make appliqué shapes and designs from leftover scraps of fabric.

NOTIONS AND STITCH SIZE

Use a size 14 needle and machine embroidery floss for appliqué sewn on by machine with a satin stitch. Either a satin stitch presser foot or a standard foot can be used. Use an embroidery needle with a large eye for hand embroidery and suitable thread. Paper-backed fusible adhesive or fabric glue can be used in place of basting stitches to secure the design before stitching.

ALTERNATIVE

Pad appropriate designs with batting to create texture and dimension. This cannot be done when a fusible adhesive is used.

PRESSING AND FINISHING

Iron the finished appliqué using a pressing cloth to protect the surface if necessary. Do not press padded appliqué.

Satin stitch appliqué

Hand-sewn folded edge appliqué

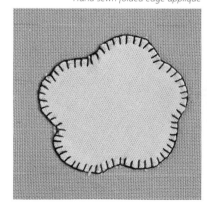

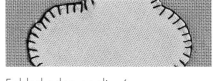

Satin stitch appliqué (using double-sided fusible adhesive)

Folded edge appliqué

1 *Iron on a paper-backed fusible adhesive to the wrong side of the fabric and cut out the appliqué shape.*

1 *Draw round a template and cut out the appliqué piece, adding ¼ in. (0.6cm) seam allowance.*

2 *Peel off the paper backing and place the appliqué design in position. With the iron, fuse it in place and allow to cool.*

2 *Stay stitch round the edge just outside the seam line. Snip and clip the raw edges and fold to the wrong side, leaving the seam line on the edge. Press and baste.*

3 *Set the sewing machine to a short-length zigzag stitch (satin stitch), and choose a suitable width to form a border on the edge of the design.*

3 *With right side facing up place the appliqué design in position and baste it to the fabric.*

4 *Sew round the edge to form a solid border around the appliqué design.*

4 *Permanently sew the design in position with a machined edge stitch or a handmade blanket stitch (or similar).*

Sewing buttons

Even non-sewers find this task necessary from time to time. The trick is to ensure buttons are sewn in place securely and neatly. As well as taking you step by step through the most useful methods, this section will look at the couture dressmaking techniques applied to covering press-studs and making buttons.

Two-hole button

Sewing buttons to a double layer of fabric gives a good anchor. A large button often has a small button sewn underneath on the wrong side for this reason. Leave a "shank" to accommodate the buttonhole's depth and use strong double thread.

1 *Secure the thread end in the fabric and take the needle through one of the buttonholes from the wrong side to the right side.*

2 *Take the needle down through the other hole, then through the fabric below. Leave a small gap between the button and the fabric.*

3 *Make several stitches as above, then take the needle round the threads between the fabric and the button to form a shank.*

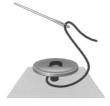

4 *To finish, on the wrong side take the needle through the threads several times to hold them together.*

GARMENT/PROJECT

Use this method to secure any two-hole button on garments, bags, or cushions.

FABRIC

Use a button with holes for all types of fabric. Always sew buttons to a double layer of cloth and reinforce with interfacing on very light fine fabrics, for example on shirt or blouse front panels or bands.

NOTIONS AND STITCH SIZE

Use strong thread, doubled. Use a hand needle with a large enough eye to take the thread but thin enough to get through the buttonholes easily. To form a shank, place a matchstick on top of the button between the holes and sew over it. Remove and pull the button up before wrapping threads between the button and fabric.

ALTERNATIVE

Use a four-hole button or one with a shank. No-sew snaps could also be used.

PRESSING AND FINISHING

Use the point of the iron to press the garment under the button. Ironing over the button will damage it.

Four-hole button

Sew buttons to a double layer of fabric and use a strong top stitch thread or double length of standard thread. Add a small button on the reverse for larger buttons. Leave a "shank" when sewing the button in place.

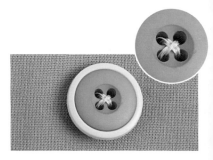

1
Secure the thread end in the fabric and take the needle through one of the buttonholes from the wrong side to the right side.

2
Take the needle over the center of the button and down through one of the other holes and through the fabric below.

3
Continue making stitches through all four holes forming a cross or two parallel bars, then take the needle round the threads beneath the button to form a shank.

4
To finish, on the wrong side take the needle through the threads several times to hold them together.

GARMENT/PROJECT
Use this method to secure any four-hole button on garments, bags, or cushions.

FABRIC
Use a button with holes for all types of fabric. Always sew buttons to a double layer of cloth and reinforce with interfacing on very light fine fabrics, for example on shirt or blouse front panels or bands.

NOTIONS AND STITCH SIZE
Use strong thread, doubled. Use a hand needle with a large enough eye to take the thread but thin enough to get through the buttonholes easily. To form a shank, place a matchstick on top of the button between the holes and sew over it. Remove and pull the button up before wrapping threads between the button and fabric.

ALTERNATIVE
Use a two-hole button or one with a shank. No-sew snaps could also be used.

PRESSING AND FINISHING
Use the point of the iron to press the garment under the button. Ironing over the button will damage it.

Button with a shank

Sew buttons with a shank to a double layer of fabric to give a good anchor. As the shank is already built in, they are easier to sew than buttons with holes.

1 *Secure the thread end in the fabric with a double stitch and take the needle through the hole in the shank. Take the needle back down through the fabric then back up to the surface again.*

2 *Make several stitches through the hole in the shank and the fabric.*

3 *Take the needle down through the fabric to the wrong side where several parallel threads lie. Take the needle under these several times and wrap them together.*

4 *Secure the thread end tightly and snip.*

GARMENT/PROJECT

Use this method to secure any button with a shank on garments, bags, or cushions.

FABRIC

Use a shank button on all types of fabric. Always sew buttons to a double layer of cloth and reinforce with interfacing on very light fine fabrics, for example on shirt or blouse front panels or bands.

NOTIONS AND STITCH SIZE

Use strong thread, doubled. Use a hand needle with a large enough eye to take the thread but thin enough to get through the holes of the button easily.

ALTERNATIVE

Use a button with holes. No-sew snaps could also be used.

PRESSING AND FINISHING

Use the point of the iron to press the garment under the button. Ironing over the button will damage it.

No-sew snaps

No-sew snaps come in various sizes to suit garments, furnishings, and camping equipment. They are clamped in position through the layers of fabric, and come in a pack with full instructions and fitting tools.

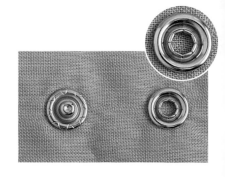

1 *Mark the positions of the snaps on the front left and right of the coat. Pierce the spot with the piercing tool on the surface and the disc below. Hit with a hammer to cut the hole required.*

2 *Place the snaps in the appropriate tools in the plastic holder and position carefully. Hit with the hammer and the rivets will snap and hold together.*

GARMENT/PROJECT

Use no-sew snaps for waterproof coats and jackets, bags, camping equipment, and jeans.

FABRIC

Use for tough heavyweight fabrics such as denim, canvas, and cotton-backed PVC.

NOTIONS AND STITCH SIZE

All you will need is a hammer!

ALTERNATIVE

Use buttons if appropriate, or sew-on snaps.

PRESSING AND FINISHING

If appropriate iron up to the edge of the snaps, but not over them.

Sewer's tip

Take care to place the correct snaps on the right and left sides of the coat (right over left for girls' clothing and left over right for boys').

Covered press-stud

For special occasion wear and jackets with large decorative non-functioning buttons, a press-stud covered with fabric is a beautiful touch. It is less obvious and is often used in couture sewing.

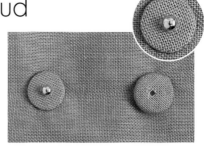

1 *Make a tiny cut through the center of a scrap of fabric and place the ball part of the stud through the hole. Attach it to its other half on the right side of the fabric.*

2 *Make tiny running stitches in a circle round the stud and gather up.*

3 *Cut away all excess fabric close to the stitches.*

4 *Repeat with the other half of the press-stud. Sew the two halves in position with tiny stitches.*

GARMENT/PROJECT

Use to attach bows and ribbons on special occasion dresses. Use to fasten jackets behind very large buttons which are only used for decoration.

FABRIC

Use only fine fabrics like silk dupion and duchesse satin. Try to avoid those which fray easily.

NOTIONS AND STITCH SIZE

Use a fine short needle with silk thread to cover press-studs and sew them in place. Choose suitably sized press-studs for the work.

ALTERNATIVE

Press-studs can be used as fastenings without being covered.

PRESSING AND FINISHING

Use a pressing cloth to protect the surface of the fabric.

Making buttons

It is possible to make buttons from fabric to match a garment. Covered buttons come in two parts, in either plastic or metal. The front part is covered with fabric and the back clips in place to complete the button and conceal all the raw edges. Buttons can also be made by covering a simple drapery ring with fabric.

Covered buttons

Use small plastic ones for fine fabrics in special occasion wear and children's clothing, and metal ones for thicker fabric as the teeth are stronger and grip better.

GARMENT/PROJECT

Use covered buttons and drapery rings when a perfect match is required. Use for special occasion wear and children's clothing. Use a contrasting color for effect.

FABRIC

Use light- and mediumweight fabrics. Use larger buttons and rings for thicker fabrics.

NOTIONS AND STITCH SIZE

Use a small needle and silk thread.

ALTERNATIVE

Paint buttons to get a color match.

PRESSING AND FINISHING

Use the point of the iron to press the garment under the button. Ironing over the button will damage it.

1 *Iron a lightweight fusible interfacing on to the wrong side of the fabric. Cut a circle of the size required for the button.*

2 *Sew a circle of running stitches (see page 28) round the edge and pull up round the button.*

3 *Place the base of the button over the shank and in position, ensuring all the raw edges are tucked inside. Press the button firmly together until the parts click in place.*

Drapery ring button

1 Use a plastic drapery ring slightly smaller than the button required.

2 Cut a circle in covering fabric twice the size of the drapery ring. Place the ring in the center of the fabric on the wrong side.

3 Secure the thread end and make tiny running stitches (see page 28) in a circle just outside the drapery ring.

4 Pull up the thread and secure the end tightly.

5 Snip away the excess fabric close to the stitches and push the raw edges toward the center of the ring.

6 Cut a circle the size of the drapery ring from the same fabric and sew a small gathering stitch (see page 38) around the outside.

7 Pull the running stitches to create a neat circle of cloth.

8 Sew the circle over the raw edges in the center of the drapery ring with regular prick stitches (see page 39) through all layers.

9 The result is a button with a center padded by the raw edges inside. Sew the underside to the fabric.

Buttonholes

Many modern sewing machines offer a selection of pre-programmed buttonholes, and will automatically make them to the correct size. But the sewer still needs to decide on the type of hole required, and where to position it. Hooks, loops, and bars are other common fasteners that the competent sewer should be well acquainted with.

Buttonhole on sheer fabric

Buttonholes are a point of stress on any garment and must be made through two layers of fabric with some form of interfacing applied.

1 *Place one or two layers of silk organza between two layers of fabric, and a strip of transparent stabilizer on the surface.*

2 *Mark the position of the buttonholes on the transparent film and baste the layers of cloth together.*

3 *Select the lightweight buttonhole, fit a fine new needle, and attach the buttonhole presser foot.*

4 *Stitch the buttonhole in place, following the instructions in the machine's manual.*

5 *Trim away the organza and the transparent film. Open the buttonhole using a seam ripper.*

GARMENT/PROJECT

Use this type of buttonhole on delicate blouses and christening robes that use small buttons.

FABRIC

Use this lightweight buttonhole for delicate, sheer fabrics made from silk, cotton, or polyester.

NOTIONS AND STITCH SIZE

The lightweight buttonhole makes a finer finish with smaller stitches and looks better on delicate and sheer fabrics. Use silk organza in a neutral color and a transparent stabilizer. Use a fine new needle (size 9 or smaller), and silk thread or machine embroidery floss which is very fine.

ALTERNATIVE

Choose a pull-on design that does not require buttonholes.

PRESSING AND FINISHING

Having trimmed away the stabilizers, press very gently, using a pressing cloth to protect the surface of the garment.

Buttonhole on stretch fabric

For buttonholes on stretch fabric use a water-soluble stabilizer and a clear tape on the surface with a gimp thread/cord under the stitches for added strength.

1 *Place a layer of water-soluble stabilizer between two layers of fabric, and a strip of transparent stabilizer on the surface.*

2 *Mark the position of the buttonholes and baste the layers of cloth together.*

3 *Select buttonhole for stretch fabric, fit a stretch needle, and attach the buttonhole presser foot.*

4 *Place the center of the gimp over the hook at the back of the presser foot and sew, covering the gimp.*

5 *Pull the gimp up to the end of the buttonhole bar and neaten the ends. Open the buttonhole with a seam ripper.*

GARMENT/PROJECT

Use this type of buttonhole on garments made from stretch or knitted fabric like jackets.

FABRIC

Use for buttonholes on a knitted or stretch fabric. Use for all weights of fabric (although the gimp can be omitted on lighter stretch materials).

NOTIONS AND STITCH SIZE

Use a ball point or stretch needle and sew with a polyester thread. Stabilize with a gimp thread (cord) and water-soluble film between the fabric layers. Use a clear strip or film on the surface to mark the buttonhole positions. Use an embroidery needle to take the gimp thread to the wrong side. Increase the stitch length slightly if a dedicated stretch buttonhole is not provided on the sewing machine.

ALTERNATIVE

Use a bound buttonhole or alternative fastening such as a zipper or toggles.

PRESSING AND FINISHING

Having neatened the gimp and trimmed away the stabilizers, press very gently, using a pressing cloth to protect the surface of the garment.

Keyhole buttonhole

 On certain garments—such as coats and tailored jackets—a keyhole or eyelet buttonhole is required as it creates a space for the shank of the button. These are normally larger buttonholes for taking larger buttons.

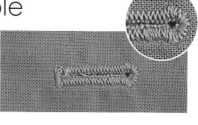

1 *Strengthen the buttonhole position between the layers of fabric with an iron-on stabilizer.*

2 *Mark the position of the buttonhole with a fabric pen or chalk and thread up the sewing machine with either buttonhole thread or strong polyester thread.*

3 *Attach the presser foot and select the eyelet buttonhole. Stitch the buttonhole in position following the instructions in the machine's manual.*

4 *When completed, open the buttonhole with a seam ripper and an eyelet punch at the keyhole end.*

GARMENT/PROJECT

 Use this buttonhole for tailored jackets and coats made from heavier fabric with larger buttons.

FABRIC

 Use for medium and heavyweight fabrics made from wool or mixed fibers.

NOTIONS AND STITCH SIZE

 Use a size 14 needle (or larger for heavier weight fabrics) and buttonhole or strong polyester thread. Use gimp to strengthen the buttonhole if required.

ALTERNATIVE

 As a decorative finish, sew a large button on the surface of the garment with a covered press stud as the fastening hidden below.

PRESSING AND FINISHING

 Press gently, using a pressing cloth to protect the surface of the garment.

Sewer's tip

Practice on spare fabric before attempting to sew on the garment. Start from the bottom and work up. Place a pin at the opposite end of the buttonhole before opening.

Machine-bound buttonhole

These attractive buttonholes can be made in matching or contrasting fabric where the edges of the buttonhole are covered in fabric rather than stitched thread.
Methods of construction vary, but this is an easy yet strong method.

1 *Fuse an iron-on interfacing to the wrong side of the fabric. Baste a bias cut rectangle of fabric on the right side.*

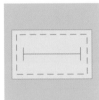

2 *Mark the shape of the buttonhole, then sew. Start in the middle of one side and pivot in the corners.*

3 *Cut the rectangle open through the center and very close into the corners without cutting any stitches.*

4 *Pull the fabric through the hole and tug at the narrow ends at the back to give a flat finish on the buttonhole front. Prick stitch (see page 39) in place.*

GARMENT/PROJECT

Use machine-bound buttonholes for tailored jackets and coats as well as bags and cushions where the fastening is a contrasting feature.

FABRIC

Use on all types of mediumweight fabrics which do not fray too badly. Stabilize with an iron-on interfacing to reduce fraying if necessary.

NOTIONS AND STITCH SIZE

Use a size 11 needle and a regular or slightly shortened straight stitch. Stabilize with a lightweight fusible interfacing to strengthen without adding bulk. Hand sew with silk thread and a fine short needle.

ALTERNATIVE

Use a corded bound buttonhole or a machine-stitched buttonhole.

PRESSING AND FINISHING

Use a pressing cloth to protect the surface of the fabric and hover gently over the finished bound buttonholes.

Hand-bound buttonhole

Putting cord inside the edges of a
bound buttonhole will make it more
defined. These buttonholes are a
suitable fastening for loose, lightweight clothing where the stress on
the front band is minimal.

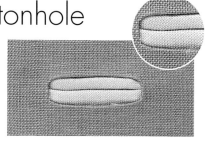

1 *Cut two small strips
of fabric and two pieces of
cord. Wrap the fabric round
the cord and baste.*

2 *Cut a small piece
of fusible film, draw on the
outline of the buttonhole,
and iron it on to the reverse
of the fabric.*

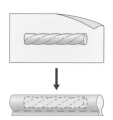

3 *With the film still
warm from the iron, cut into
the corners and fold back
the edges to reveal a
letterbox shape.*

4 *Arrange the cord-
filled strips inside the
letterbox and sew with small
stitches around the edge to
hold them in place.*

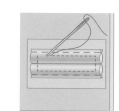

GARMENT/PROJECT

Use this type of corded buttonhole on
fastenings which do not receive a lot
of stress. Ladies' loose-fitting cotton
blouses and tops would be suitable,
or bags where the fastening is a non-
functioning feature.

FABRIC

Light- and mediumweight fabrics
made from natural fibers like cotton
and linen work well. Avoid fabrics
which fray easily. Use contrasting or
matching colors for corded bound
buttonholes.

NOTIONS AND STITCH SIZE

Use narrow cotton cord for best
results. Use a fine short needle and
matching silk thread for basting and
hand stitching for best results.

ALTERNATIVE

Use a machine-bound buttonhole
(see opposite).

PRESSING AND FINISHING

Iron from the wrong side with the
buttonhole placed down over a soft
towel. This will prevent it from
becoming flat.

Corded button loop

Button loops filled out and strengthened with cord make a suitable fastening for ball-shaped buttons on keyhole necklines, cuffs, and wedding dresses. Covering the cord with fabric gives an exact match for a garment.

GARMENT/PROJECT

Use corded button loops as fastenings on wedding bodices, cuffs, necklines, and edge-to-edge jackets. Use them with round buttons, covered buttons, or toggles.

FABRIC

Can be made from any fabric, but must be cut on the bias for a smooth result.

NOTIONS AND STITCH SIZE

Use a suitable width of cord for the sewing task and stitch with the help of a zipper or piping foot attachment. A size 11 needle will suit most fabrics, and the stitch length should be shortened to allow more give when pulling through.

ALTERNATIVE

Use a self-filled Rouleau loop (see page 179, opposite).

PRESSING AND FINISHING

It is not necessary to press the finished loops.

Making the covered cord

1 *Cut a length of bias fabric to the length required. It must be wide enough to cover the cord with extra for a seam allowance. Cut a piece of cord twice this length.*

2 *With the right side of the fabric on the inside enclose the cord in the fabric. Only half the cord will be covered.*

3 *Attach the zipper or piping foot and stitch adjacent to the cord. Pivot and stitch across through the cord just before the end of the fabric covering the cord.*

4 *Trim off the excess seam allowance to approximately ⅛ in. (0.3cm) and ease the fabric over the remainder of the cord.*

Making a self-filled Rouleau loop

Making the loops

1 *The loops can be cut individually and used singly. Chalk a line to mark the position of the fastening line and fold the loop, placing it on the line with the raw edges toward the edge. When stitched in place the loop will face outward over the edge to take the button.*

2 *The entire covered cord can be looped along the length of the fastening line and stitched in place. Baste parallel lines on the fabric as a guide and fold the cord into loops, ensuring they are evenly spaced and equally sized. Baste the loops in position and sew the inner ends (toward the edge) in place. Remove the basting and fold the loops to the outer edge.*

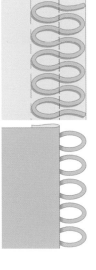

1 *Cut a length of bias strip approximately 1 in. (2.5cm) wide and fold it lengthways with the right side on the inside.*

2 *Shorten the stitch length and sew close and parallel to the folded edge. The distance from the edge will be determined by the width of the loop required. Stitch a second line of stitching adjacent to the first in the seam allowance.*

3 *Without trimming any excess, turn the loop through with a Rouleau turner tool or a large blunt needle threaded with double thread and secured to one end. The result is a tube padded with the seam allowance.*

Eyelet hole

Eyelet holes can be made by hand sewing with buttonhole stitch, selecting an eyelet stitch on the sewing machine, or using metal eyelets hammered in place. Use them for belts and lacings.

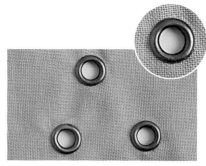

Metal eyelets

By hand

1 *Mark the eyelet position and punch a small hole using a stiletto.*

2 *Using blanket stitch (see page 31) or buttonhole stitch (see page 32), sew over the raw edges of the eyelet hole. Keep the stitches close and even to give a strong neat edge.*

Metal eyelets

1 *Mark the eyelet position and punch a small hole using a stiletto.*

2 *Place the stud through the hole from front to back. Use a punching tool to squeeze the stud and flatten it over the edges of the hole.*

Sewing machine eyelets

GARMENT/PROJECT

 Use eyelets on belts and for threading lace or ribbon on bodices and bags.

FABRIC

 Use on all types and weights of fabric. Fuse an iron-on interfacing to the inside of delicate fabrics to add strength.

NOTIONS AND STITCH SIZE

 Use a medium or small needle and strong thread. Keep stitches even and close to make a strong edge.

ALTERNATIVE

 Send part-made garments to companies who provide an eyelet-making service, or stitch at home with a sewing machine. Follow the instructions in the manual.

PRESSING AND FINISHING

 No special instructions for pressing and finishing.

Hooks and eyes or bars

Use hooks and eyes where edges meet, and hooks and bars where one edge covers the other. These fasteners are available in various sizes and are often used as closures at necklines and waistbands.

Hook and eye

Pant hook and bar

Sewing hooks and eyes

1 *Position the hooks and eyes/bars accurately to give a flat finish.*

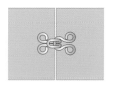

2 *Use a small needle with strong thread. Secure the thread end in the fabric below the hook, eye, or bar. Bring the needle up through the center and stitch over the metal circle, catching the fabric below. Work round the circle, covering it with small straight stitches.*

Making thread bars or loops

1 *Run two or three threads for the bar in the position required.*

2 *Start at one end and make blanket or buttonhole stitches over the threads until covered. Secure the thread end carefully.*

GARMENT/PROJECT

Use hooks and eyes on edge-to-edge jacket fronts or similar edge fastenings. Use hooks and bars where the fronts overlap, for example on the waistband of a skirt or pants.

FABRIC

Use on all weights and types of fabric, but choose a suitable size.

NOTIONS AND STITCH SIZE

Use strong thread and a small needle.

ALTERNATIVE

Make thread bars or loops rather than using metal ones.

PRESSING AND FINISHING

No special instructions.

Zippers

This chapter shows how to insert zippers into different types of garment. Various methods are included, and suggestions are given on choice depending on the fabric and the type of garment being constructed. Follow the diagrams and the instructions to see how easy they are to sew in place.

Quick zipper

The quick zipper is a lapped method where one side of the fabric covers the teeth. It is easy to get a neat result as the visible stitching is made on flat fabric before the zipper is in place.

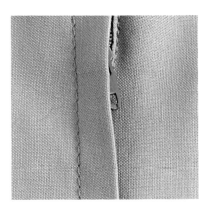

1 *Use a large seam allowance of 1 in. (2.5cm). Pin the right sides together then stitch the seam, leaving a long gap for the zipper.*

2 *Press the seam open and with right sides up, mark the position of the top stitching with a ruler and chalk. Sew along this line before the zipper is put in.*

3 *Place over the zipper, and pin and baste the folded seam allowance to the right edge of the zipper tape. Stitch in place close to the zipper teeth.*

4 *Place the already top-stitched left side of the seam over the zipper, and pin the zipper tape to the seam allowance. Turn the work over and stitch these two layers together.*

GARMENT/PROJECT

Use this quick method if you are afraid of making wobbly top stitching. Use for skirts and children's clothing.

FABRIC

Use on most fabrics, but medium-weight woven cotton will be easiest for handling.

NOTIONS AND STITCH SIZE

Choose a needle suitable for the fabric (see page 14) and good matching cotton or polyester thread for the top stitching. Lengthen the stitch slightly for the top stitching. Always select a good quality zipper in a suitable weight for the fabric.

ALTERNATIVE

Use a lapped method of insertion.

PRESSING AND FINISHING

Press lightly from the right side over the zipper placement, using a pressing cloth to protect the fabric surface.

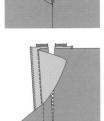

Centered zipper

With this method the seam meets over the zipper and the teeth are centered under the seam, with stitching equidistant on either side.

GARMENT/PROJECT

Use this centered method for zippers inserted in the center back of garments or for bags and cushions.

FABRIC

Use for all types and weights of fabric.

NOTIONS AND STITCH SIZE

Use a needle suitable for the fabric (see page 15) and good matching cotton or polyester thread for the top stitching. Lengthen the stitch very slightly for the top stitching. Always select a good quality zipper in a suitable weight for the fabric.

ALTERNATIVE

Use a concealed/invisible zipper (see pages 194–5) or the hand-finished zipper method (see pages 188–9).

PRESSING AND FINISHING

Press lightly from the right side over the zipper placement, using a pressing cloth to protect the fabric surface.

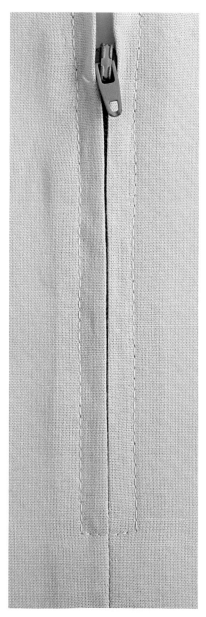

1 Neaten the raw edges of the seam by your preferred method.

2 Machine stitch the seam from the base of the zipper position to the hem line.

3 Select the longest straight stitch and machine the remainder of the seam with long basting stitches.

4 Press the seam open and lay it face downward. Place the zipper face downward over the seam part sewn with basting stitches. Ensure that the teeth are centered over the basting stitches, and that the zipper tape is level with the top edge of the fabric. Pin and baste through all layers.

5 Turn the work over and attach a zipper foot to the sewing machine. Work from the bottom of the zipper and stitch each side in turn, adjusting the zipper foot accordingly. To stitch, start at the base of the zipper (below the teeth) and stitch three or four stitches ⅜ in. (1cm) away from the seam. Leave the needle down, raise the presser foot, and pivot 90 degrees. Lower the presser foot and stitch parallel to the zipper teeth to the top edge.

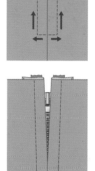

6 Remove all the basting stitches.

Sewer's tip

To stitch smoothly past the zipper tag, stitch as close to it as possible, leave the needle down in the fabric and raise the presser foot. Ease the zipper tag past the needle and out of the way. Snip some of the basting stitches if necessary. Lower the presser foot and continue stitching.

Lapped (offset) zipper

A lapped zipper has the teeth offset with only one edge covering them. Use this method for side fastenings.

GARMENT/PROJECT

Use a lapped zipper method for fastening skirts and dresses in the side seam. Use it also for cushions.

FABRIC

Use on all fabrics.

NOTIONS AND STITCH SIZE

Use a needle suitable for the fabric (see page 14) and good matching cotton or polyester thread for the top stitching. Lengthen the stitch very slightly for the top stitching. Always select a good quality zipper in a suitable weight for the fabric.

ALTERNATIVE

Use a concealed/invisible zipper or the quick zipper alternative.

PRESSING AND FINISHING

Press lightly from the right side over the zipper placement, using a pressing cloth to protect the fabric surface.

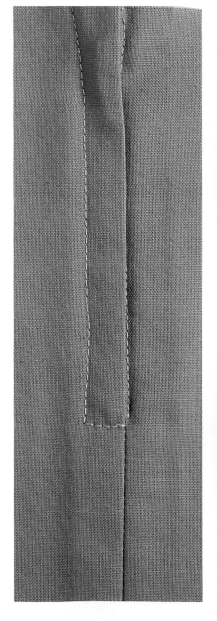

1 Neaten the
raw edges of the seam
by your preferred
method.

2 Machine stitch
the seam from the base
of the zipper position to
the hem line.

3 Press the seam
open, including the
unsewn part.

4 With right
sides uppermost, place
the right folded seam
allowance over the
zipper tape adjacent to
the teeth. Pin and baste
in place.

5 Attach a zipper
foot to the sewing
machine and stitch the
right side of the zipper in
place. Stitch from the
bottom of the zipper to
the top.

6 Place the left
folded edge to the right
edge (over the teeth of the
closed zipper). Pin and
baste together through
all layers to the left of
the teeth.

7 Start at the base
of the zipper, below the
teeth, and stitch the left
side of the zipper in place.

Sewer's tip

To stitch smoothly past the zipper tag, stitch up
as close to it as possible, leave the needle down
in the fabric, and raise the presser foot. Ease the
zipper tag past the needle and out of the way.
Lower the presser foot and continue stitching.

Hand-finished zipper

This method has the look of a hand-finished zipper but the strength of a machine-inserted zipper. It looks beautiful on dresses for special occasions and works well on some fabrics which are difficult to sew, like velvet and lace.

GARMENT/PROJECT

Use this strong hand-finished zipper placement on special occasion dresses to give a couture effect.

FABRIC

Use on all fabrics but velvet, lace, beaded, and silk materials would benefit from this method.

NOTIONS AND STITCH SIZE

Use fine hand and machine needles when working on delicate fabrics. Use silk thread for the prick stitching.

ALTERNATIVE

Use a concealed or invisible zipper.

PRESSING AND FINISHING

Press lightly from the right side over the zipper placement, using a pressing cloth to protect the fabric surface.

1 Neaten the raw edges of the seam by your preferred method.

2 Machine stitch the seam from the base of the zipper position to the hem line, and press the seam open.

3 Mark the seam line on the neck edge with a tiny snip.

4 With right sides uppermost, place the right folded seam allowance over the zipper tape adjacent to the teeth. Pin the folded edge to the tape and turn the work over.

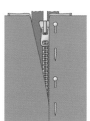

5 From the wrong side, re-pin the tape to the seam allowance. Attach the zipper foot to the sewing machine and stitch the zipper to the fabric ¼ in. (0.6cm) from the teeth.

6 Turn the work back to the right side. Pull the zipper to the left and iron it lightly to make it lie flat with ¼ in. (0.6cm) of zipper tape showing between the teeth and the fabric.

7 Place the left folded edge over the right edge, matching the snips on the center back neck edge. The teeth are completely concealed. Pin this left seam edge to the left side of the zipper tape.

8 Turn the work to the wrong side and re-pin the zipper tape to the seam allowance only. With the zipper foot attached, stitch the zipper tape along the pin line.

9 Work from the right side with a fine sharp needle and matching silk thread. Prick stitch the back seam to the zipper tape with stitches ⅜ in. (1cm) apart to finish the zipper.

Pants zipper

This fly-fronted zipper can be used for pants, shorts, or skirts. For men the zipper is inserted with the left side over the right, and for ladies the right is placed over the left.

GARMENT/PROJECT

Use this method for pants, shorts, and skirts.

FABRIC

Use for medium- and heavyweight fabrics.

NOTIONS AND STITCH SIZE

Use a strong needle size 14 or above. A jeans needle will cope with layers of very heavy fabric. Select a good quality zipper—either a pants zipper or a normal zipper for lighter-weight pants. On thicker fabrics lengthen the stitch.

ALTERNATIVE

A fly-fronted zipper is used most often for pants. Alternatively fasten ladies' pants with a concealed/invisible zipper in the side seam.

PRESSING AND FINISHING

No special instructions.

Sewer's tip

Reverse this method for men's pants.

1 Neaten the raw edges of the seam by your preferred method.

2 Machine stitch the seam from the base of the zipper position to the crotch.

3 Select the longest straight stitch and machine baste the zipper opening of the seam. Press the seam open.

4 With the wrong side up, place the zipper face down with the teeth centered over the basted seam.

5 Pin the left side of the zipper tape to the seam allowance of the seam on the left, approximately ⅛ in. (0.3cm) from the edge of the tape. Pin through the seam allowance only.

6 Attach the zipper foot and machine along the pin line.

7 Pull the zipper tape to the right and pin it through all layers.

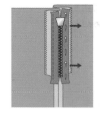

8 Turn the work over and re-pin from the right side. Baste the layers together and top stitch around the zipper, starting from the base and working to the waistline.

9 Make a guard to cover the zipper on the inside from spare fabric. It should be the length of the zipper plus ½ in. (1.2cm) x 4 in. (10cm) wide.

10 With the zipper right side facing up, place the guard under the zipper teeth on the right with 1¼ in. (3.2cm) showing. Turn the work over and pin, tack, and machine to the seam allowances.

Open-ended zipper

Open-ended or separating zippers come apart completely and are used for jackets and bags. There are now lightweight varieties available for evening and bridal bodices.

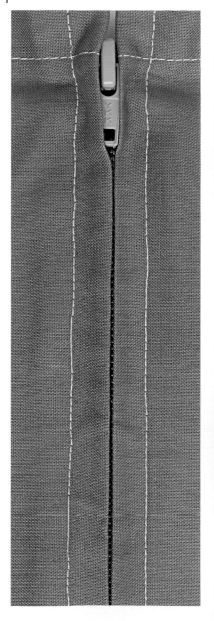

GARMENT/PROJECT

Use a separating zipper for jackets, boned bodices, and bags.

FABRIC

Use an open-ended zipper for medium- and heavyweight fabrics when making jackets and bags. Use for bodices made from silks, brocades, or velvets (although these will probably be heavily interlined).

NOTIONS AND STITCH SIZE

Select an open-ended zipper in a suitable weight for the task. Use a size 14 needle or larger to sew through the fabric layers and zipper tape. The fabric may need to be stabilized before inserting the zipper.

ALTERNATIVE

To separate an opening completely use buttons, toggles, or poppers.

PRESSING AND FINISHING

There is no need to iron over the zipper if it is finished with edge or top stitching, as this will keep it flat.

1 *Machine baste the seam where the zipper is to be inserted.*

2 *Press the seam open, and place the closed zipper face down over the basted seam. Pin and baste the tape in place.*

3 *Remove the basting stitches from the seam and separate the zipper. It will be easier to work with two independent pieces when stitching the zipper in position.*

4 *Attach the zipper foot and top stitch the zipper in place, stitching from the right side. Start from the base and stitch approximately ⅜ in. (1cm) from the teeth. Complete both sides.*

Hints and tips

Try mixing open-ended zippers for children's novelty coats. Buy two zippers of the same length and type in contrasting colors and mix them. This, teamed with a bright selection of fabric panels, will make for a fun coat and a child who will never get lost in a crowd!

Some fabric will stretch when applying a separating zipper, for example fleece or sweat shirt fabric. Stabilize the edges with a fusible tape or stay stitching before sewing the zipper in place.

Conceal a separating zipper under the panels in a corset or bodice, and have laces or covered buttons for decoration only. It will be quicker to put on and will be comfortable and secure when worn.

Concealed/invisible zipper

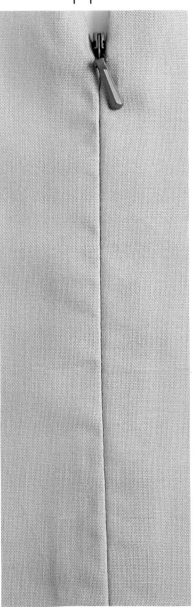

When concealed or invisible zippers are in place they are indeed invisible. They are easy to insert if the correct presser foot is fitted to the machine as the teeth are tilted out of the way while the stitches are sewn in the exact position required. As the zipper is hidden within the seam it is not essential to use an exact color match.

GARMENT/PROJECT

Use an invisible or concealed zipper in skirts, ladies' pants, and dresses. Use where an obvious fastening is not suitable for the design.

FABRIC

Use on velvet and other pile fabrics where top stitching is not appropriate.

NOTIONS AND STITCH SIZE

Choose a size 11 needle or larger, depending on the weight of fabric. Use a normal zipper foot and a concealed zipper foot for best results.

ALTERNATIVE

A hand-finished zipper placement can be used instead of a concealed method.

PRESSING AND FINISHING

Treat the zipper when fitted as part of the seam, and iron accordingly.

1 *Neaten the raw edges of the seam, retaining the ⅝ in. (1.5cm) seam allowance.*

2 *In a contrasting color, hand baste the position of the seam line on both sides for the length of the zipper.*

3 *Keep the two parts of the seam separate, and pin the zipper to each edge with right sides facing. Note the position of the teeth in relation to the seam line.*

4 *Attach the normal zipper foot to the machine, and stitch the zipper close to the outside edge of the tape. This line of stitching will hold the zipper in the correct position when stitching close to the teeth.*

5 *Fit the invisible zipper foot to the machine and adjust the zipper teeth, feeding the row of teeth into the groove of the invisible zipper foot whilst stitching. The stitches will be formed right at the base of the teeth.*

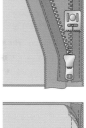

6 *Remove the concealed zipper foot and replace it with the normal zipper foot. Find the position of the last stitches at the base of the zipper and, with right sides together, sew the remainder of the seam from the base of the zipper to the hem. The normal zipper foot allows the stitches to be made from the last zipper stitches.*

Sewer's tip

The seam is sewn after the zipper is inserted to prevent a bubble or wrinkle from forming at the base of the zipper.

Textile
Directory

Choosing the right fabric for your project is key, and once you do, you'll need to know how to get the best from it. Follow the advice in this section to make sure you pick the right needles, stitches, and finishes.

Note: The stitch lengths in this section are given in millimeters and in the number of stitches per inch. Please check your user manual to determine which method your machine uses.

Lightweight fabrics

Lightweight fabrics can be described as fine, sheer, soft, or crisp, and are made from natural or synthetic fibers. They are thin and light, and often need careful handling.

General advice

- Check the full length of the cloth for flaws before cutting out. It cannot be returned to the store if you spot these after you have started cutting.

- Cut out with sharp shears to give a smooth cutting edge.

- Use a rotary cutter for small pattern pieces.

- Use bridal pins and place them in the seam allowance to limit damage to the fabric.

- Use a fine, standard needle or Microtex needle for sewing.

- Sew with machine embroidery floss if necessary as it is very fine.

- A crisp textured fabric will be easier to work with than a softer one.

- For straight stitch, use a straight stitch sole plate. This prevents the fabric from being pushed down into the body of the machine.

- Do not start sewing a fine fabric on the edge. Start just in from the edge to avoid the fabric being pushed down into the body of the machine.

- Pull gently in front of and behind the needle when stitching to eliminate puckering.

- Wind bobbins slowly. Fast-wound bobbins are taut and can cause seams to pucker.

Gauze

Gauze is a loosely woven, plain weave, cotton cloth. It is unbleached or white in color and comes in various weights. The best quality gauze is made from strong, fine woven yarns, while cheaper gauze is thinner and sized to add stiffness (but this washes out).

GARMENT/PROJECTS

Use to make drapes, or as an underlining.

CUTTING OUT

Gauze can be bought in 36 in. (91cm) and 45 in. (114cm) width. It has no nap, so follow the grain when cutting out. Lay the fabric on a flat surface and use sharp, long-bladed scissors to cut.

SEWING SUGGESTIONS

Sew with a size 9 needle and a stitch length of 10–12 stitches per 1 in. (2.5mm). Use cotton thread, and if necessary stiffen with spray starch. When sewing garments, stay stitch curved seams and necklines, and use plain seams (see page 123) or French seams (see page 124).

Voile

Voile is a sheer, transparent fabric which is both thin and light. It is similar to cotton lawn and organdie. It's a plain weave fabric made with highly spun yarns giving it a soft crispness, and is made from cotton or synthetic fibers.

GARMENTS/PROJECTS

Drapes, blouses, and dresses—lining where necessary.

CUTTING OUT

Cover the cutting table with a bedsheet to prevent the voile from moving. Do not fold the voile and cut out in a single layer. Secure with long pins and cut out using very sharp shears.

SEWING SUGGESTIONS

Sew with a size 9 needle and a stitch length of 12–15 stitches per 1 in. (2mm). Use a good quality fine polyester thread. A straight stitch foot plate and presser foot may make machine stitching easier. When making up, use hairline seams (see page 125) or French seams (see page 124) which will be lighter and less visible on such a sheer fabric.

Organdie

Silk organza

Organdie is a sheer, crisp, plain weave cloth made from very fine cotton yarns woven to produce a smooth and fine fabric. It creases easily but modern finishes can help to prevent this.

Organza is a thin, sheer fabric made from highly spun, long silk fibers. It has a stiff finish, making it suitable for clothing and for supporting weaker fabrics.

GARMENTS/PROJECTS

Blouses or shirts. The crispness of the fabric makes some styles more suitable than others.

GARMENTS/PROJECTS

Special-occasion wear and bridal gowns, blouses, shirts, and hats; window dressings, drapes, and gift bags. Also an excellent interlining to strengthen and stabilize loosely woven woolen skirts.

CUTTING OUT

Easier to cut than more softly draping fabrics, but care should still be taken. There is no obvious right or wrong side, so be consistent when cutting. Use long fine pins and sharp shears, or a rotary cutter and board.

CUTTING OUT

Easier to cut than more softly draping fabrics but take care: there is no obvious right or wrong side, so be consistent when cutting out. Use long fine pins and sharp shears, or a rotary cutter and board.

SEWING SUGGESTIONS

Sew with a fine size 9 needle and a short stitch length of 12 stitches to 1 in. (2–2.5mm). A straight stitch foot plate and presser foot will ease machine stitching. Use fine cotton thread for machining and hand sew with silk. Construct garments with French seams (page 124) or hairline seams (page 125); if underlining is required use organdie.

SEWING SUGGESTIONS

Sew with a size 9 needle and a short stitch length of 12 stitches to 1 in. (2.5mm). A straight stitch foot plate and presser foot may make machine stitching easier. Use fine thread for machining and hand sew with silk thread. Construct garments with French seams (see page 124) or hairline seams (see page 125); if underlining is required use organza.

Silk habotai

Habotai is a very soft, fine silk in a smooth, plain weave. It drapes softly but can cling to the body.

GARMENTS/PROJECTS

Lining, camisoles, nightdresses, and robes. As it is soft and made from a natural fiber it absorbs moisture which makes it comfortable next to the skin.

CUTTING OUT

Cover the cutting table with a bedsheet to prevent the silk slipping. Cut out in a single layer. Secure with long pins and cut with sharp shears; or place on a cutting board and use a rotary cutter.

SEWING SUGGESTIONS

Sew silk habotai with a size 8 machine needle and a stitch length of 12–15 stitches to 1 in. (2–2.5mm). Choose a standard or Microtex needle and use a straight stitch foot plate and presser foot. Use good quality fine cotton, silk, or polyester thread. When sewing up use French seams (see page 124). Hem with a narrow, double-folded hem or a hand-sewn rolled hem (see page 146). For linings use plain seams (see page 123).

Cotton lawn

Cotton lawn is a fine, smooth, plain weave fabric. It has a soft crisp finish and absorbs moisture, making it comfortable to wear.

GARMENTS/PROJECTS

Dresses, blouses, and lightweight skirts; lingerie and nightdresses; children's clothes.

CUTTING OUT

Use long-bladed scissors, or lay the fabric on a board and cut with a rotary cutter if the pattern pieces are small enough. Hold in place with long sharp pins.

SEWING SUGGESTIONS

Sew with a fine size 9 machine needle and a short stitch length of 12 stitches to 1 in. (2.5mm). A straight stitch foot plate and presser foot may make machine stitching easier. Use fine cotton thread for machining and hand sew with silk. Make up with plain seams (see page 123) or French seams (see page 124). Pull the fabric in front of and behind the presser foot while sewing, to prevent wrinkling. Pressing will also help; or use three-thread serged seams.

Cotton batiste

Thai silk

Batiste is a soft, fine, lightweight fabric woven in a plain weave. It is similar to lawn and organdie, and can be made from wool or polyester fibers. It is sometimes called cambric.

GARMENTS/PROJECTS

Dresses, blouses, and children's clothes; perfect for antique or heirloom sewing.

CUTTING OUT

Use long-bladed scissors, or lay the fabric on a board and cut with a rotary cutter if the pattern pieces are small enough. Hold the fabric in place with long sharp pins.

SEWING SUGGESTIONS

Sew with a fine size 9 machine needle and a short stitch length of 12 stitches to 1 in. (2.5mm). A straight stitch foot plate and presser foot may make machine stitching easier. Use fine cotton thread for machining and hand sew with silk. Make up with French seams (see page 124), pulling the fabric in front of and behind the presser foot while sewing to prevent wrinkling. Pressing will also help. Alternatively, use three-thread serged seams.

Thai silk is a lightweight, plain weave fabric with an uneven surface created by slubs in the weft threads. It has a lustrous surface and is similar to silk dupion.

GARMENTS/PROJECTS

Eveningwear and bridal gowns; cushions, pillows, and window dressings.

CUTTING OUT

The appearance of Thai silk can change depending on the light reflecting on its lustrous surface. It is therefore necessary to cut out all pattern pieces in the same direction to avoid differences of color. Use sharp shears for cutting out.

SEWING SUGGESTIONS

Use a size 9 machine needle and a stitch length of 10 stitches to 1 in. (2.5mm). Use good quality fine cotton thread on the sewing machine and silk thread for hand stitching. Use plain seams (see page 123) pressed open and neatened with a serger. Neaten hems with a Hong Kong finish (pages 136–7) before turning up.

Lining

Lining fabrics can be made from silk fibers, manmade, or synthetic fibers. They are all lightweight, thin, and have a slippery surface, which eases putting on and taking off garments. The weave can be plain or satin.

GARMENTS/PROJECTS

Jackets, coats, dresses, skirts, pants, and handbags are all lined to enclose the raw edges within.

CUTTING OUT

Cut each pattern piece from a single layer to prevent the shapes being distorted. Cover the cutting table with a bedsheet to prevent slipping. Follow the same grain as the outer shell of the garment. Use lots of pins to hold the fabric in position and cut with shears.

SEWING SUGGESTIONS

Sew with a size 9 machine needle and a stitch length of 12 stitches per 1 in. (2.5mm). Choose a standard or Microtex needle and use a straight stitch foot plate and presser foot. Use fine cotton, silk, or polyester thread. When sewing up use plain seams (see page 123) pressed open.

Georgette

Georgette is a lightweight fabric, similar to chiffon, with a dull crêpe surface texture. It is highly twisted, giving it more body and stiffness than would be expected for its weight

GARMENTS/PROJECTS

Loose-fitting blouses, shirts, dresses, and gathered skirts.

CUTTING OUT

Cover the cutting table with a cotton sheet to prevent the georgette from slipping. Do not fold the fabric and cut out in a single layer. Secure with long pins and cut out using sharp shears.

SEWING SUGGESTIONS

Use a size 8 universal point or Microtex machine needle and a stitch length of 12–15 stitches to 1 in. (2mm). Use a straight stitch foot plate and presser foot for best results. Use good quality fine cotton, silk, or polyester thread. When sewing up use French seams (see page 124) as they are light and enclose the raw edges neatly. Hem with a narrow, double folded hem or a hand-sewn rolled hem (see page 146).

Mediumweight fabrics

These are probably the easiest weight of material to work with, especially if they are stable as they will neither stretch nor slip when being handled. Often used for "home dec" projects, mediumweight fabrics are also suitable for skirts, pants, shirts, and similar garments.

General advice

- Check the full length of the cloth for flaws before cutting out. It cannot be returned to the store if you spot these after you have started cutting.

- Cut small pieces to experiment with for washing, ironing, and stitching.

- Cut with sharp shears to give a smooth edge. Short scissors will give a ragged cut.

- Pre-shrink by steaming or washing if necessary.

- Iron fabric from the wrong side or use a pressing cloth to protect the surface.

Muslin

Muslin is a coarse, unbleached, plain weave fabric made from cotton or a cotton blend. It varies in quality but is generally unfinished and undyed. It is inexpensive and creases badly.

GARMENTS/PROJECTS

Use for trial garments to check for fit, and to cover mattresses and sofas/chairs as a base for the outer upholstery fabric.

CUTTING OUT

Easy to handle and cut—no specific instructions are required.

SEWING SUGGESTIONS

Use a size 11 machine needle and normal stitch length of 10 stitches to 1 in. (2.5mm) for most tasks. Use steam when pressing seams. Use plain seams (see page 123), flat fell seams, or mock flat fell seams (see page 126).

Poplin

Poplin, generally made from cotton, has a crossways ribbed texture on the surface. This is due to heavier weft yarns. It is a strong, durable fabric which is easy to iron and does not wrinkle.

GARMENT/PROJECTS

Dresses, jackets, pants, and skirts, as well as "home dec" projects.

CUTTING OUT

Easy to handle and cut out—no specific instructions are required.

SEWING SUGGESTIONS

Use a size 11 machine needle and normal stitch length of 10 stitches to 1 in. (2.5mm) for most projects. Use plain seams (see page 123), flat fell seams, or mock flat fell seams (see page 126), and a good quality cotton thread. Use steam when pressing seams.

Damask

Damask refers to the pattern created in the weave by a jacquard loom, and the resulting fabric can be made from various fibers including silk, cotton, linen, and blends. The pattern is in a single color but is seen in the contrasting matte base and long, shiny threads as they float on the surface of the fabric.

GARMENTS/PROJECTS

Dresses, jackets, pants, and skirts as well as "home dec" projects. Traditionally, damask weaves were used for table linen and also for bedding.

CUTTING OUT

Damask fabric, especially if made in a natural fiber, is easy to cut. Check the pattern carefully and cut in one direction and symmetrically so that reflecting sides of a garment are the same.

SEWING SUGGESTIONS

Use a size 11 machine needle and normal stitch length of 10 stitches to 1 in. (2.5mm) for most projects. Use plain seams (see page 123), flat fell seams, or mock flat fell seams (see page 126), and good quality cotton thread. Use steam when pressing seams.

Cheesecloth

Traditionally used to wrap cheese, this cotton cloth is loosely woven with a crinkled texture with a crêpe appearance. The construction of the cloth combined with its natural fiber content make it an ideal choice for hot-weather garments.

GARMENTS/PROJECTS

Popular during the 1970s as casualwear for shirts, blouses, and dresses. Use it today for window dressings and drapes.

CUTTING OUT

Pre-wash to shrink the fabric and iron lightly. Place a bedsheet on the cutting table to "hold" the fabric in place and cut out pattern pieces in a single layer.

SEWING SUGGESTIONS

Use a size 11 machine needle, a stitch length of 10 stitches to 1 in. (2.5mm), and cotton thread. Use spray starch to stiffen and make handling and sewing easier. Construct with plain seams (see page 123) or French seams (page 124).

Chintz

Chintz is made from closely woven, plain weave cotton. It is crisp with a glaze or sheen on the surface because of a finish created by calendaring or a resin. Chintz can be plain or printed.

GARMENTS/PROJECTS

Furnishing and "home dec" projects; lightweight chintz for dresses and blouses.

CUTTING OUT

Lay flat on the cutting surface and use long-bladed scissors. Hold the pattern pieces in place with pins.

SEWING SUGGESTIONS

Use a sharp size 11 machine needle and a stitch length of 10 stitches to 1 in. (2.5mm). Use good quality cotton or polyester thread, and plain seams (see page 123) or flat fell seams (see page 126) for construction.

Sateen

Sateen is a woven cotton cloth with a satin weave. The long surface threads reflect light as a dull shine. If the threads are mercerized this strengthens them and improves their luster.

GARMENTS/PROJECTS

Drape linings and bedding.

CUTTING OUT

Easy to handle and cut out.

SEWING SUGGESTIONS

Use a size 11 machine needle and a stitch length of 10 stitches to 1 in. (2.5mm). Use good quality cotton thread and plain seams (see page 123) or flat fell seams (see page 126) for construction, or sew with a serger.

Cashmere

Flannel

Cashmere comes from the fine, soft undercoat of the Kashmir goat. It is used on its own or mixed with other fibers. It may be knitted or woven into fabric and produces a soft, warm, luxurious cloth.

GARMENTS/PROJECTS

Woven cashmere for coats, jackets, skirts, and scarves; knitted cashmere for sweaters, cardigans, and dresses.

CUTTING OUT

Cut all pattern pieces in the same direction as the fabric has a nap. Use long pins or weights to secure the pattern and cut with shears.

SEWING SUGGESTIONS

Use a standard size 11 machine needle and a stitch length of 10 stitches to 1 in. (2.5mm) for woven fabrics. Use a ball point or stretch needle for knitted cashmere. Choose good quality polyester or silk thread. Use plain seams (see page 123) pressed open for lined garments or serged seams for unlined woven and knitted clothing. Finish hem edges with a Hong Kong finish or "Seams Great" (see pages 136–7) and lock stitch (see page 36) to hold in place. Dry clean only.

Flannel is a durable fabric made from cotton or wool fibers in a plain or twill weave. The surface is normally brushed or napped on one or both sides. Flannelette is a light- to mediumweight cotton flannel used for bedding, pyjamas, and nightdresses as the napped surface makes them feel warm.

GARMENTS/PROJECTS

Suits, coats, dresses, and pants; flannelette to make sheets, pillowcases, and nightwear.

CUTTING OUT

Cut all pattern pieces in the same direction as the fabric has a nap. Use long pins to secure the pattern and cut with shears.

SEWING SUGGESTIONS

Use a size 11 machine needle and normal stitch length of 10 stitches to 1 in. (2.5mm) for most projects. Use plain seams (see page 123), flat fell seams, or mock flat fell seams (see page 126), and quality cotton or polyester thread. Apply steam when pressing seams. Neaten edges with a serger, double fold hems and top stitch in place.

Gabardine

Gabardine is a firm, closely woven fabric made from worsted wool, cotton, synthetic, or mixed fibers. It is woven in a twill weave giving diagonal ribs on the surface of the cloth. It drapes well and does not wrinkle.

GARMENTS/PROJECTS

 Tailored garments like jackets, pants, skirts, and coats; bag making.

CUTTING OUT

 Cut all pattern pieces in the same direction. Use long pins or weights to secure and cut with shears.

SEWING SUGGESTIONS

 Use a size 11 or 14 machine needle and a stitch length of 10 stitches to 1 in. (2.5mm) for most projects. Use plain seams (see page 123), flat fell seams, mock flat fell seams (see page 126), or welt seams (see page 127), and good quality cotton or polyester thread. Use steam when pressing seams. Neaten edges with binding (see pages 152–3) or a three-thread serger stitch (see page 65); double fold hems and top stitch in place.

Worsted wool

A worsted yarn is one where long fibers have been combed and highly twisted to give a smooth, strong finish. This yarn is then woven in a plain or twill weave to create a resilient fabric.

GARMENTS/PROJECTS

 Depending on the weight of the cloth, use for coats, jackets, dresses, pants, and skirts.

CUTTING OUT

 Lay flat and folded double on the cutting surface. Pin or use weights to secure the pattern pieces. If in doubt about whether the surface has a nap cut the pieces in the same direction.

SEWING SUGGESTIONS

Use a size 11 machine needle and a stitch length of 10 stitches to 1 in. (2.5mm). Use good quality silk, polyester, or cotton thread in a close color match. Use plain seams (see page 123) pressed open, and line jackets, skirts, and part line pants. Elsewhere, serge, bind, or Hong Kong finish raw edges (see pages 136–7).

Linen

Linen is made from the stems of the flax plant, which are processed to release the fibers, and the resulting yarns are woven into a strong, crisp cloth. The fabric can be woven in plain, twill, and damask. It wrinkles badly but is cooling to wear in hot temperatures.

GARMENTS/PROJECTS

Depending on the weight: blouses, shirts, jackets, pants, coats; traditional-style bed linen with antique stitch decoration.

CUTTING OUT

Use shears or a rotary cutter and board.

SEWING SUGGESTIONS

Use size 9 or 14 machine needles, a stitch length to suit the cloth weight, and quality cotton thread. Use plain seams (see page 123), flat fell seams, mock flat fell seams (see page 126), or welt seams (see page 127). Use steam when pressing seams. Neaten edges with binding (see pages 152–3) or a three-thread serger stitch. For antique style stitching, use a wing needle and machine blanket stitch (see page 143).

Hemp

Hemp comes from the stems of the *Cannabis sativa* plant. The stems are processed to release the fibers and the resulting yarns are woven into a strong, coarse cloth. It looks and handles much like linen.

GARMENTS/PROJECTS

Jackets, pants, shirts, skirts, dresses, and bags.

CUTTING OUT

Hemp fabric is strong and requires sharp long-bladed scissors for cutting.

SEWING SUGGESTIONS

Hemp is an easy fabric to handle and sew. Use a size 14 machine needle and a stitch length of 10 stitches to 1 in. (2.5mm). For top stitching lengthen this to 8 stitches to 1 in. (3mm). Use good quality cotton thread (linen if you can get it). Use plain seams (see page 123), flat fell seams, mock flat fell seams (see page 126), or welt seams (see page 127). Use steam when pressing seams. Neaten edges with binding (see pages 152–3) or a three-thread serger stitch (see page 65).

Microfiber

A fine, synthetic fiber filament, Microfiber is suitable for fine fabric and heavier weights. The strong yarns withstand different treatments, and create a variety of finishes, including suede and sand. The surface does not pill like some synthetics. It drapes well but does not cling or crease, making it a versatile modern cloth.

GARMENTS/PROJECTS

Soft and draping designs; (depending on the finish) tablecloths, carseat covers; sportswear.

CUTTING OUT

Assume the fabric has a nap and cut all pieces in the same direction. Use sharp, long-bladed scissors. Use strong fine pins within the seam allowance or weights.

SEWING SUGGESTIONS

Sew with a new size 9 machine needle and with a stitch length of 15 stitches to 1 in. (2mm). Choose a Microtex needle, quality polyester thread, and sew with a walking foot or straight stitch foot. Mock flat fell seams (see page 126) are a good choice. Press with a dry iron.

Silk dupion

Silk dupion is a crisp, woven fabric with an uneven surface created by slubs in the yarn. Unlike many other silk fabrics it is easy to handle, although it does crease.

GARMENTS/PROJECTS

Eveningwear and bridal gowns; dresses, skirts, pants, and suits; hats, lampshades, cushions, and handbags.

CUTTING OUT

The color of silk dupion can vary depending on how light reflects on it, so cut out all pattern pieces in the same direction. Use sharp shears.

SEWING SUGGESTIONS

Use a size 9 or 11 machine needle and a stitch length of 10 stitches to 1 in. (2.5mm). Use good quality cotton thread on a sewing machine and silk thread for hand stitching. Use plain seams (see page 123) or serge the seams with a three-thread stitch (see page 65). Neaten the hem with a Hong Kong finish (see pages 136–7) or, if shaped, use a faced hem (see pages 138–9). Piping works well on dupion fabric and adds detail to seams and edges (see page 155).

Crêpe de Chine

Crêpe de Chine is a soft, crêpe textured, plain weave cloth which is available in light and medium weights. It is often made from silk but synthetic fibers are also used today.

GARMENTS/PROJECTS

Dresses, tops, blouses, camisoles, and soft jackets—depending on the weight of the cloth.

CUTTING OUT

Cover the cutting table with a cotton sheet to prevent the crêpe de Chine from slipping on a smooth surface. Cut in a single layer and use sharp shears.

SEWING SUGGESTIONS

Use a size 9 or 11 (standard or Microtex) machine needle and a stitch length of 10–12 stitches to 1 in. (2.5mm). Use good quality cotton or silk thread on the sewing machine and silk thread for hand stitching. Join fabric panels with a serger or with French seams (see page 124).

Raw silk (NOIL)

Raw silk is made from the shorter, poorer quality silk fibers. It is woven and has a dull surface finish. It frays badly.

GARMENTS/PROJECTS

Jackets, shirts, skirts, and dresses which are loose and not closely fitted; drapes.

CUTTING OUT

As raw silk frays badly, cut larger seam allowances. Secure pattern pieces with long pins and use sharp shears.

SEWING SUGGESTIONS

Sew raw silk with a standard size 11 or 12 machine needle, and 10 stitches to 1 in. (2.5mm). Serge the edges of all fabric pieces before sewing up to prevent fraying. Use plain seams (see page 123) or flat fell seams (see page 126), and fold up hems twice, then top stitch.

Gingham

Recognized by its checks, gingham is generally made from cotton in a light- to mediumweight fabric. Some of the yarns are dyed, and the resulting plain weave fabric creates squares or stripes of white and a color—traditionally blue.

GARMENTS/PROJECTS

Shirts, blouses, and dresses; children's clothing; "home dec" projects like cushions and bedroom or kitchen drapes.

CUTTING OUT

Treat as any light- to mediumweight cotton fabric but consider the stripes and checks when cutting out to ensure that these match at seams and openings. Secure the pattern pieces with pins and use notches and pattern markings as a guide to match panels.

SEWING SUGGESTIONS

Use a size 11 standard machine needle and a stitch length of 10 stitches to 1 in. (2.5mm). Sew with cotton or polyester thread and use plain seams (see page 123), flat fell seams (see page 126), or welt seams (see page 127). Hand basting (see page 46) helps to match checks. For hems, fold up twice and top stitch.

Batik

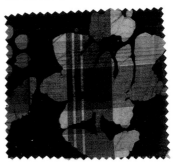

Batik fabric is so called because of the form of resist dyeing that is used to decorate it. Wax is poured on to areas of the cloth, which is then dyed. The process is repeated several times to build up pattern and color before the wax is removed. Normally light- to medium-weight plain weave cotton cloth is used.

GARMENTS/PROJECTS

Dresses, shirts, blouses, skirts, or for patchwork and quilting designs.

CUTTING OUT

As batik is a light- to mediumweight cotton fabric it is easy to handle and cut out.

SEWING SUGGESTIONS

Use a size 9 or 11 standard machine needle and a stitch length of 10 stitches to 1 in. (2.5mm). Sew with a good quality cotton or polyester thread and use plain seams (see page 123) or three- or four-thread serged seams (see pages 65–6).

Heavyweight fabrics

These can be difficult fabrics to cut out and handle, being stiff or thick and bulky. In general, you should use a stronger, larger needle and sew with slightly longer stitches for best results.

General advice

- Check the full length of the cloth for flaws before cutting out. It cannot be returned to the store if you discover these after you have started cutting.

- Always use sharp, long-bladed scissors to give a smooth edge.

- If pins are not long enough use weights to secure pattern pieces.

- Cut in a single layer rather than folding the fabric if it is too thick.

- Use a larger machine needle (size 14 or above) and increase the stitch length.

- Lift the pressure from the foot when sewing.

- A walking foot is sometimes helpful when sewing thick layers.

- Use a "humper jumper"—an H-shaped gadget which is placed under the presser foot (front or back) to level the foot and ease stitches over thick seams, for example, jean hems.

Canvas

Corduroy

needle
cord

heavy
corduroy

Canvas is a heavy-duty, tightly woven fabric generally in a twill weave. It is a strong and rigid cloth varying in weight but too heavy for making clothes. It's made from cotton, linen, hemp, and jute.

Corduroy is a woven fabric recognized by the ridges which run the length of the cloth. These can vary from fine needle cord to broader whale cord. Cord is made from cotton and the pile surface gives it a nap. It is very strong and hard-wearing.

GARMENTS/PROJECTS

Covering deckchairs and director's chairs; bag making; "home dec" projects.

CUTTING OUT

Cut out in a single layer and use sharp long-bladed scissors. Use weights rather than pins, which are difficult to push through the canvas.

SEWING SUGGESTIONS

Use a strong jeans machine needle to sew canvas (size 16 or 18). Long stitches—7 or 8 to 1 in. (3mm) —and very strong thread are best for sewing seams and finishing edges. Use plain seams (see page 123) pressed open with the raw edges neatened with three-thread serging (see page 65).

GARMENTS/PROJECTS

Jackets, pants, skirts; children's clothing; handbags; beanbags, cushions.

CUTTING OUT

Cut all pattern pieces in the same direction as light reflects off the surface pile, making it appear different shades. Cord is harder wearing if the pile direction is downward, but a richer shade of color is achieved when the pile direction is upward. Use sharp shears.

SEWING SUGGESTIONS

For lighter weight needle cord use a size 11 needle and an average stitch length of 10 stitches to 1 in. (2.5mm). For heavier weights use a larger size 14 needle and 7 stitches to 1 in. (3mm). When sewing seams together a "humper jumper" (see opposite) is useful to ease the presser foot over the layers of material.

Velveteen

Velveteen is similar to velvet but the pile is shorter and created by the weft threads. It is made from cotton and cotton blend and has a dull surface. It is easier to work with than velvet.

GARMENTS/PROJECTS

Coats, jackets, skirts; children's clothes; bags, beanbags, and drapes. It is more versatile than velvet for eveningwear, being more durable and easier to care for.

CUTTING OUT

Cut all pattern pieces in the same direction as light reflects off the surface pile, making it appear different shades. Velveteen is harder wearing if the pile direction is downward, but a richer shade of color is achieved when the pile direction is upward. Use sharp shears.

SEWING SUGGESTIONS

Sew with a size 12 machine needle and about 10 stitches to 1 in. (2.5mm) with quality cotton thread. Sew along the pile and use a walking foot to prevent the top layer of velveteen from creeping over the lower layer. As with velvet, concealed or invisible zippers are a good choice.

Denim

light
denim

heavy
demin

Denim is a very strong cotton fabric made in a twill weave that generally has blue warp threads and white weft threads, giving it its characteristic appearance.

GARMENTS/PROJECTS

While remaining strong, denim can be treated to soften it, making it suitable for a wider range of sewing projects. Use heavyweight denim for jeans, jackets, straight skirts, bags, and upholstery; lighter weight for shirts, dresses, and softer skirt styles.

CUTTING OUT

Problems arise from its toughness; when placing a paper pattern on to denim it may be easier to use weights rather than pins. Use sharp, long-bladed scissors.

SEWING SUGGESTIONS

Choose a size 12, 14, or 16 jeans machine needle depending on the fabric weight. Sew with 10 stitches to 1 in. (2.5mm) with a cotton or polyester thread. Use plain seams (see page 123), flat-fell seams, or mock flat-fell seams (see page 126). Use a "humper jumper" (see page 214) when joining seams.

Fleece

Synthetic fleece provides warmth without weight and is a comfortable and durable fabric. It is often treated to give better finishing qualities, such as anti-pilling, and comes in a range of weights. It doesn't fray and has a degree of stretch.

GARMENTS/PROJECTS

 Perfect winter clothing with simple lines, such as jackets, sweaters, blankets, hats, and scarves.

CUTTING OUT

 Check for right and wrong sides to make the most of any special finishes. Mark all pieces with chalk on the wrong side before sewing up. Use sharp scissors or a rotary cutting blade.

SEWING SUGGESTIONS

 A serger copes well with the stretch of the fabric. Use a three-thread (see page 65), four-thread (see page 66), or flatlocked seam (page 68). With a sewing machine use a walking foot and a stretch stitch or narrow zigzag (see page 53). Finish the seam allowances together and top stitch through all layers. Use a twin needle and a walking foot to hem (see pages 142–3).

Wool tweed

Wool tweed is a woven fabric traditionally made from coarse homespun wool. It is normally made from two or more colors of yarn, creating checks or pattern. It is a warm fabric but its coarse texture is not comfortable next to the skin.

GARMENTS/PROJECTS

 Ideal for jackets, waistcoats, and coats. It can be used for pants or skirts but must be lined for comfort and to avoid seating. Tweed handbags, men's scarves, and hats are also popular.

CUTTING OUT

 Cut tweed in a single layer if checks are to be matched accurately. Use sharp shears.

SEWING SUGGESTIONS

 Due to the thickness of the cloth, a longer stitch length is necessary—approximately 8 to 1 in. (3mm)—and a large size 14 machine needle. Plain seams pressed flat are most appropriate (see page 123). Since the garment is likely to be lined, the raw edges do not need to be neatened. Use corded keyhole buttonholes (see page 175) or bound buttonholes (see page 176).

Silk tweed

Silk tweed is a loosely woven cloth with a rough surface as it is made with yarns spun from shorter silk fibers. Like wool tweed, the pattern is created by the colored woven threads. It is warm and comfortable to wear but often needs the support of an underlining.

GARMENTS/PROJECTS

Smart jackets and coats.

CUTTING OUT

Has a tendency to ravel. If necessary, over stitch the edges with a serger after cutting to prevent fraying. Take note of the surface pattern to ensure that seams match well. Use sharp, long-bladed scissors. Cut an underlining in silk organza. Baste to the wrong side of the silk tweed, then treat as one.

SEWING SUGGESTIONS

Sew with a standard size 12 needle and 12 stitches to 1 in. (2.5mm). Use silk or quality polyester thread. Use plain seams and press open (page 123). If the edges haven't been neatened with a serger, use a Hong Kong finish or "Seams Great" (pages 136–7), or binding (pages 152–3).

Tartan

A traditional Scottish woolen cloth, tartan threads or yarns are dyed and then woven into cloth in bands of color, creating plaids or checks.

GARMENTS/PROJECTS

Skirts, dresses, pants, jackets, and blankets, as well as the traditional kilt.

CUTTING OUT

Cuts and sews like other woven wool fabrics but its distinctive checks or plaids make it necessary to match it carefully when joining seams. Cut all pieces in one direction, taking note of notches and pattern markings. Cut in a single layer to ensure all plaids match accurately.

SEWING SUGGESTIONS

Use a standard size 14 needle and 8 stitches to 1 in. (3mm). Use silk thread or good quality polyester thread. Use plain seams (see page 123) and neaten with a Hong Kong finish or "Seams Great" (see pages 136–7), or binding (see pages 152–3). Use a pressing cloth to protect the surface of the fabric while ironing.

Camel hair

From the undercoat of the Bactrian camel, this hair can be used on its own or combined with other wools, and woven or knitted to make cloth. It is soft and warm.

GARMENTS/PROJECTS

Blankets, coats, jackets, scarves; knitted camel hair for sweaters and cardigans; coarser hair is made into rugs.

CUTTING OUT

Cut all pattern pieces in the same direction as the fabric has a nap. Use long pins or weights to secure the pattern and cut with shears.

SEWING SUGGESTIONS

Use a standard size 11 machine needle and 10 stitches to 1 in. (2.5mm) for woven fabrics. Use a ball point or stretch needle for knitted camel hair. Sew with quality polyester or silk thread. Use plain seams (see page 123) pressed open for lined garments, or neaten seams in unlined woven and knitted clothing with a serger. Apply a Hong Kong finish or "Seams Great" (pages 136–7), and use a lock stitch (page 135) to hold in place.

Bouclé

Bouclé refers to the surface texture of a fabric which has curled loops, of which there are many varieties. Bouclé yarn (normally wool) is curled and twisted, and when woven or knitted creates the loopy texture.

GARMENTS/PROJECTS

Jackets and coats; knit into sweaters and cardigans. Its novelty surface makes it suitable for simple designs.

CUTTING OUT

May have a tendency to ravel if loosely woven. Other bouclé fabric may have a long pile on the surface. In this case, cut the body of the fabric from the wrong side with short-bladed scissors and pull the surface threads apart.

SEWING SUGGESTIONS

Use a standard size 12 machine needle for woven bouclé and a stitch length of about 10–11 stitches to 1 in. (2.5mm). Use a stretch or ball point machine needle for knitted bouclé and sew with a serger, or use a stretch stitch (see page 55) or narrow zigzag (see page 53) if using a sewing machine.

Mohair

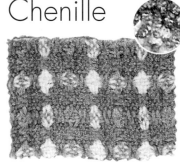

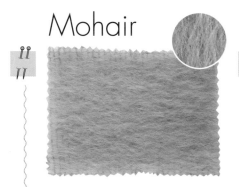

Mohair—derived from the Angora goat—is soft, silky and warm, producing a beautiful lustrous fabric. It is durable and resilient, but due to the expense of the fiber is often blended with others.

GARMENTS/PROJECTS

Jackets and coats.

CUTTING OUT

Cut all fabric pieces in the same direction. Unless the fabric is thick, use pins rather than weights to secure the pattern pieces.

SEWING SUGGESTIONS

Use a standard size 11 or 12 machine needle with about 10 stitches to 1 in. (2.5mm). Sew with plain seams and neaten with a serger (see page 65), a Hong Kong finish, or "Seams Great" (see pages 136–7). Use silk or polyester thread for machining and hand sew with silk thread. Protect the surface of the fabric with a pressing cloth, or iron from the wrong side.

Chenille

Chenille yarn has a velvety texture, so the resulting cloth (which is normally knitted) has a soft, tufted pile. It is a thick and warm fabric made from wool, cotton, or synthetic fibers.

GARMENTS/PROJECTS

Sweaters, cardigans, and jackets.

CUTTING OUT

Tends to ravel. Cut with shears, then over stitch the raw edges with a serger before stitching the pieces together. Cut all pieces in the same direction.

SEWING SUGGESTIONS

Sew with a standard or stretch machine needle in a size 12. Stitch length should be 10–11 stitches to 1 in. (2.5mm). Choose a good quality polyester or cotton thread and use plain seams pressed open. Stabilize shoulder seams with a stay tape (see page 129), and take care when ironing seams and hems that the pile does not become flattened. Press lightly from the wrong side using steam.

Toweling

Toweling, or terry cloth, is a cotton fabric with loops, sometimes on one, but normally on both, sides. The increased surface area created by the loops makes it highly absorbent, ideal for its principal use in towels.

GARMENTS/PROJECTS

Towels, robes, and beachwear.

CUTTING OUT

When cutting out toweling tiny bits of pile remain when the pieces are cut. Shake each piece to release these and vacuum them up before continuing.

SEWING SUGGESTIONS

Sew toweling with a standard size 12 machine needle and a stitch length of 8–9 stitches to 1 in. (2.5mm). Use good quality cotton thread. Use a four-thread serged seam (see page 66) or plain seams (see page 123) neatened with a serger to join fabric pieces.

Upholstery fabric

There are many varieties of upholstery fabric but it is always strong, tough, and hard-wearing, which makes it difficult to sew.

GARMENTS/PROJECTS

Loose covers (slip covers) for chairs and sofas; cushions, heavy drapes, shades; and even bags.

CUTTING OUT

Problems may arise from its toughness and it may be easier to use weights rather than pins. Cut in a single layer and use sharp long-bladed scissors. Take care when matching pattern at seams and use notches and pattern markings to help.

SEWING SUGGESTIONS

Use a large (size 16 or 19) jeans machine needle as it is strong with a sharp point. Use strong upholstery thread and choose plain seams (see page 123). Piping can be added for detail within the seams (see page 155).

Stretch fabrics

Stretch fabrics are often knitted in construction which allows the fabric to move when pulled, although it is also possible for woven fabrics to stretch due to the addition of Lycra. Such fabrics may stretch slightly or extensively, across the cloth or both across and lengthwise. Some garment designs require stretch in both directions, while others need stability married with stretch in only one direction.

General advice

- Check the full length of the cloth for flaws before cutting out. It cannot be returned to the store if you discover these after you have started cutting.

- Check if the pattern requires one-way or two-way stretch for the design to work.

- Pull the fabric to see how much it stretches and how well it recovers.

- Check that the fabric is not twisted before cutting out.

- Place the pattern pieces according to the direction of stretch required.

- Use stretch needles or ball point needles as these slip between the threads rather than splitting them.

- Polyester thread has a slight "give" and works well for most stretch fabrics.

- Cut small pieces of fabric and experiment by washing, ironing, and stitching.

- Sergers cope well with stretch due to the differential feed. If using a sewing machine a walking foot helps to avoid any rippling which would otherwise occur.

Cotton jersey
(T-SHIRT FABRIC)

Sweatshirt fabric

Cotton jersey is a lightweight knitted cloth often used to make T-shirts. Its knitted construction enables it to stretch, and the combination of this and the cotton fiber makes it comfortable to wear. It has a smooth surface and drapes well.

Also jersey cotton, this is a heavier weight of knitted fabric with a smooth plain knit surface on the right side and a brushed surface on the wrong side. It is warm and comfortable to wear.

GARMENTS/PROJECTS

Sweatshirts, sports pants, casual zippered jackets; loose-fitting garments.

GARMENTS/PROJECTS

T-shirts, tops, and dresses; sports clothing and underwear.

CUTTING OUT

Ensure that the fabric is not twisted and is flat. Check whether the pattern requires a one-way or two-way stretch fabric. Use a rotary cutter or sharp scissors.

CUTTING OUT

Ensure that the fabric is not twisted and is flat. Check whether the pattern requires a one-way or two-way stretch fabric. Use a rotary cutter or sharp scissors.

SEWING SUGGESTIONS

Choose a stretch or ball point machine needle in a suitable size (12 or 14). A serger copes well with stretching; or select a stretch stitch or narrow zigzag (see page 53) and attach a walking foot (see page 19). Neaten the raw edge with a three-thread serged stitch (see page 65) and fold up. Top stitch from the right side with a twin needle and attach the walking foot to prevent rippling. Alternatively, finish cuffs and hems with a rib or band (see page 158). Stabilize shoulder seams with tape (see page 129).

SEWING SUGGESTIONS

Choose a stretch or ball point machine needle in a suitable size. A serger copes well with stretching; or select a stretch stitch or narrow zigzag (see page 53) and attach a walking foot (see page 19). To hem cotton jersey, neaten the raw edge with a three-thread serged stitch and fold up. Top stitch from the right side using a twin needle and attach the walking foot to prevent rippling (see page 142). Stabilize shoulder seams with tape (see page 129).

Spandex (LYCRA)

slight
stretch

very
stretchy

Spandex is a modern synthetic fiber with great stretch and recovery. It can be used in fabrics of both knitted and woven construction in varying proportions, and is also used in suiting to retain shape.

GARMENTS/PROJECTS

Sportswear, dancewear, lingerie, and underwear; tailored garments like jackets, pants, and straight skirts.

CUTTING OUT

Use long, sharp pins or weights to secure the pattern, and cut with sharp, long-bladed scissors or a rotary cutter.

SEWING SUGGESTIONS

Sew with a stretch or ball point machine needle in size 11 or 12 with quality polyester thread. A serger copes well with stretching; or select a stretch stitch (see page 55) or narrow zigzag (see page 53) and attach a walking foot (see page 19). Neaten the raw edge with a three-thread serged stitch (see page 65) and fold up. Top stitch from the right side using a twin needle and attach the walking foot to prevent rippling (see page 142). Stabilize shoulder seams with tape (see page 129).

Woolen jersey

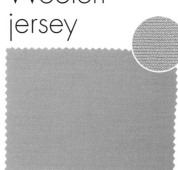

Thicker knitted fabric made from wool or wool blends can be hand knitted or constructed on a machine with a similar appearance. It ravels badly once cut.

GARMENTS/PROJECTS

Sweaters, cardigans, and loose-fitting casual jackets.

CUTTING OUT

Once cut, over sew the fabric edges with a serger before sewing the pieces together to prevent them from raveling.

SEWING SUGGESTIONS

Sew with a size 12 to 14 stretch or ball point needle and polyester thread. Sew with a serger as this copes well with the stretch in the cloth. Alternatively, select a stretch stitch (see page 55) or narrow zigzag (see page 53) and attach a walking foot (see page 19) to the sewing machine. Finish cuffs and hems with a rib or a folded band (see page 158). Stabilize shoulder seams with tape (see page 129).

All-over stretch lace

Slinky Knit

(KNITTED SYNTHETIC FABRIC)

All-over stretch lace is made from blends of synthetic and elasticated threads in a knitted construction.

GARMENTS/PROJECTS

Lingerie; eveningwear; dance or ice-skating costumes.

CUTTING OUT

Cover the cutting table with a bedsheet to prevent slipping. Use safety pins if the mesh or lace is open and pins won't hold. Consider the design when placing the pattern pieces.

SEWING SUGGESTIONS

Choose a stretch needle and sew seams with a serger set for rolled hemming as this copes well with stretching and creates a narrow seam. Use strong polyester thread. If using a sewing machine use a stretch stitch (see page 55) and attach a walking foot to prevent rippling. If joining stretch lace to other stretch fabric neaten the raw edges and use a lapped seam (see page 128). Stabilize shoulder seams with tape (see page 129). Finish necklines and hems with a folded band of the lace fabric and use the quarter pinning method (see page 150).

These are knitted fabrics, with two-way stretch, made from synthetic fibers mixed with spandex (Lycra). Slinky Knit drapes beautifully, doesn't wrinkle, and is comfortable to wear.

GARMENTS/PROJECTS

Simply shaped dresses, skirts, and tops will benefit from the drape of the fabric. Casual clothes which pull on and off with no need for closures.

CUTTING OUT

Cover the cutting table with a bedsheet to prevent the fabric from slipping, and do not allow it to hang off the table as this distorts it. Use sharp scissors.

SEWING SUGGESTIONS

Use a size 10 or 12 stretch needle and good quality polyester thread. Serge seams for best results or use a sewing machine fitted with a walking foot attachment (see page 19) and sew with a stretch stitch (see page 55) or narrow zigzag (see page 53). Finish necklines with a folded band (see page 158) and hem with a twin needle and walking foot (see page 19).

Velour

Velour is the knitted equivalent of velvet. It has a thick soft pile with a surface sheen. It looks like velvet but has more drape due to its knitted construction.

GARMENTS/PROJECTS

Simply shaped dresses, skirts, and tops will benefit from the drape of the fabric.

CUTTING OUT

Cover the cutting table with a cotton sheet to prevent the fabric from slipping, and do not allow it to hang off the table as this distorts it. Place with pile sides together and use sharp scissors.

SEWING SUGGESTIONS

Use a size 12 stretch needle and good quality polyester thread. Use a serger to make seams or sew with a stretch stitch (see page 55) or short narrow zigzag (see page 53) and a walking foot (see page 19). Avoid ironing if possible but if necessary use a needle board or a piece of the same fabric to protect the pile. If a zipper is required, use a concealed or invisible type (see page 194) as this becomes part of the seam and there is no need for top stitching.

Powernet

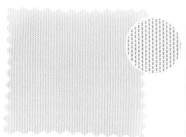

Powernet contains a high proportion of spandex in its construction, giving it excellent four-way stretch and recovery.

GARMENTS/PROJECTS

Bras, knickers, corset panels, and girdles.

CUTTING OUT

Use weights rather than pins and cut with a rotary cutter with a self-healing mat beneath, or sharp shears.

SEWING SUGGESTIONS

Use a size 12 stretch machine needle. Choose a stretch stitch (see page 55) or a short, narrow zigzag (see page 53) for seaming and sew with good quality polyester thread. Neaten bras and knickers with edging elastic using the quarter pin method (see pages 150–1).

Special occasion fabrics

These include decorative, delicate, hand-finished, or expensive fabrics which might make sewers particularly nervous of cutting and sewing. Such material needs to be handled as lightly as possible and laid flat, to avoid the need for ironing.

General advice

- Check the full length of the cloth for flaws before cutting out. It cannot be returned to the store if you discover these after you have started cutting.

- Take time to study the pattern before you start to cut out.

- Cut off small swatches and experiment with washing, ironing, and stitching.

- Iron from the wrong side or use a pressing cloth to protect the surface.

- Use a dry iron unless you are confident that water marks won't remain.

- Unstable or delicate fabrics should be placed in a single layer on a cotton bed sheet for cutting out to avoid the fabric distorting.

Lace

Lace is a fine, open cloth with a pattern. It's made with threads of silk, cotton, or synthetic fibers. Some laces are hand crocheted, while others are embroidered threads or cords on a net background.

GARMENTS/PROJECTS

Evening and bridal wear; lingerie and nightdresses; babies' clothes; edging lace for trimming garments.

CUTTING OUT

Check for the right side (has the most texture). Cover the cutting table with a cotton sheet in a contrasting color to the lace. If the lace is to be pieced together (see page 148) take notice of pattern markings and notches, and cut extra-wide seam allowances.

SEWING SUGGESTIONS

Use size 9 machine needles for delicate lace and size 11 for heavier. Use a cotton or polyester thread, or for fine lace try machine embroidery floss. Use a fine seam finish like a French seam (see page 124) or narrow serged seam (see page 64), or lap the lace panels to be joined and zigzag along a prominent line of the design (see page 148).

Broderie anglaise

This is a form of lace or cut work with a pattern stitched on a lightweight white cotton background and small areas of the fabric removed. It does not need the same careful handling as many other laces.

GARMENTS/PROJECTS

Shirts, blouses, young children's clothing, cushions, drapes, and bedding.

CUTTING OUT

Take notice of the design and match notches and pattern markings if necessary.

SEWING SUGGESTIONS

Use a standard size 11 machine needle and cotton or polyester thread. Sew seams with a serger or use plain seams (see page 123). Broderie anglaise often has a scalloped, finished edge along the length of the fabric—cut this off and use it to finish cuffs and hems.

Velvet

cotton
velvet

synthetic
velvet

Velvet is a woven fabric with a dense pile on one side. Traditionally made from silk, these days it's usually made from cotton, polyester, viscose, and/or acetate.

GARMENTS/PROJECTS

Jackets, skirts, bodices, special occasion garments; "home dec" projects; bags.

CUTTING OUT

Cut in the same direction to prevent shade differences. For better-wearing qualities cut with the pile downward; for a richer color cut with the pile upward.

SEWING SUGGESTIONS

Sew with a standard size 12 machine needle and quality polyester or cotton thread. Sew with 8–10 stitches to 1 in. (3mm) and use a walking foot to prevent the top layer creeping over the lower one. Raise the presser foot several times while sewing a seam to let it settle. Sew along the pile and not against it. Concealed or invisible zippers become part of the seam (see page 194), and top stitching a zipper in place will flatten the pile. Avoid ironing, but if necessary use a velvet board or a spare piece of velvet.

Beaded or sequined

Luxury fabric patterned with sequins or beads and embroidery is expensive, so more care is required when working with it.

GARMENTS/PROJECTS

Bridal wear; dresses, jackets, bodices for special occasions. hand- or clutch bags.

CUTTING OUT

Cover the cutting surface with a cotton sheet and lay the fabric face down in a single layer. Cut only the backing fabric using short-bladed needlework scissors. Try not to cut the sequins or beads as this will damage the scissors.

SEWING SUGGESTIONS

Carefully remove the sequins and beads from the seam allowances without cutting the threads away. Attach a zipper foot and stay stitch just inside the seam allowance. Use a size 12 machine needle and—continuing to use the zipper foot—sew plain seams (see page 123) to join the fabric pieces. Finger press the seams open and hand sew the beads and sequins (removed from the seam allowance) in any gaps along the seam. Line the finished garment. Do not iron.

Brocade

Brocade is a crisp, bulky fabric with a surface design woven on a jacquard loom. The design is created by raised surface threads which give a pattern on both sides of the cloth. Metallic threads are often incorporated into the design.

GARMENTS/PROJECTS

Elegant evening jackets and waistcoats; cushions and drapes.

CUTTING OUT

Take note of the brocade design and cut all pieces in the same direction if necessary and match where seams join. Use sharp shears.

SEWING SUGGESTIONS

Use a size 12 to 16 machine needle depending on the toughness of the brocade. Use a longer stitch of about 8 stitches to 1 in. (3mm). Sew with plain seams (see page 123) and line the garment or use a Hong Kong finish (see pages 136–7). Before ironing the fabric, test a piece to see how it reacts. Iron from the wrong side or finger press the seams open.

Taffeta

Taffeta is a crisp, plain woven fabric with a surface sheen. Traditionally made from silk, today manmade and synthetic fibers are often used. Sometimes the warp and weft threads are of different colors to give an iridescent effect.

GARMENTS/PROJECTS

Full evening gowns and party wear; lampshades and cushions.

CUTTING OUT

Use weights, or pins within the seam allowances, and cut all pieces in the same direction. Work quickly and handle the fabric as little as possible to avoid the raw edges raveling.

SEWING SUGGESTIONS

Use a fine sharp machine needle (size 9) and about 10 stitches to 1 in. (2.5mm). As the fabric frays badly, overcast the edges with a serger (see page 65) immediately after cutting out and sew plain seams (see page 123). Alternatively, use French seams (see page 124) to conceal edges. Use a dry iron or a steam one with care as water can spot.

Lamé

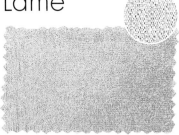

Lamé can be either woven or knitted from metallic threads. It has a luxurious, glittery appearance but ravels badly.

GARMENTS/PROJECTS

Evening and party wear—dresses, skirts, tops, and so on. It is also useful for theatrical, dance, or skating costumes, and has many craft applications.

CUTTING OUT

Use shears or a rotary cutter and mat. Cutting lamé may blunt scissors.

SEWING SUGGESTIONS

Use a new fine size 9 needle (a less-than-sharp needle can pull and damage the fabric threads). Sew with about 10 stitches to 1 in. (2.5mm) and use French seams (see page 124) for straight edges and neaten curved seams with "Seams Great" (see page 136).

Duchesse satin

Duchesse satin, made from silk or synthetic fibers, has a beautiful shiny surface due to the satin weave. It is a heavier weight than satins used for lingerie and linings, but is just as lustrous and slippery to work with.

GARMENTS/PROJECTS

Wedding gowns and evening dresses; purses and clutch bags.

CUTTING OUT

Cut all pieces in the same direction. Use long, sharp pins within the seam allowance to secure the pattern and cut with sharp shears. Keep pieces flat as folding leaves permanent creases. Iron as little as possible with a dry iron.

SEWING SUGGESTIONS

Handle the fabric lightly. Sew with a new size 9 needle, 10–12 stitches to 1 in. (2.5mm), and use plain seams (see page 123) or French seams (see page 124). Underline skirts with net or silk organza to give added body. Use a false or faced hem (see page 138) and secure hand stitches to the underlining. Tiny stitches show up on the shiny, satin surface.

Crêpe-backed satin

This has a softer handle than duchesse satin with one smooth, lustrous side and a dull, crêpe side. Either or both sides can be used in a garment. Traditionally made from silk, it is now often made from manmade and synthetic fibers.

GARMENTS/PROJECTS

Blouses and dresses. Mixing both sides of the cloth has an attractive effect.

CUTTING OUT

Cover the cutting table with a bedsheet to avoid the satin from slipping. Cut all pieces in the same direction. Use long, sharp pins and sharp shears.

SEWING SUGGESTIONS

Sew with a new size 9 needle (a less-than-sharp needle can pull and damage the fabric threads on the satin side). Sew with 10–12 stitches to 1 in. (2.5mm) and use plain seams (see page 123) or French seams (see page 124). Fold up the hem edge twice, and top stitch and edge stitch for a sharp finish (see page 160).

Chiffon

Chiffon is a fine, sheer fabric with a soft, open weave. It has a floating quality and drapes nicely. It is generally made from synthetic fibers today, although silk chiffon is still available.

GARMENTS/PROJECTS

Simply shaped styles with few seams. Gathered skirts, loose tops and dresses; as an overlayer.

CUTTING OUT

Difficult to cut as it moves so readily. Cover the cutting board with a cotton sheet to help it stick. Ensure that the fabric is square with the edge of the table before attaching the pattern. Use long-bladed, sharp scissors.

SEWING SUGGESTIONS

Sew with a new size 9 needle. Sew with 10–12 stitches to 1 in. (2.5mm) and machine embroidery floss. Join panels with French seams (see page 124) as they are light and enclose the raw edges neatly. Use a straight stitch throat plate and a straight stitch presser foot, and start each seam just in from the edge. Hem with a rolled edge (see page 146).

Net and tulle

Net is a mesh of threads making a crisp, light, openweave fabric. Tulle is generally a finer mesh with a slightly softer handle.

GARMENTS/PROJECTS

Net has a stiff quality, ideal for creating volume. As well as being a dress fabric, it's frequently used as an underlining to create body without weight to a full skirt or underskirt. Tulle is more often used for veils or in multiple layers to make floaty bridal and evening skirts.

CUTTING OUT

Use weights or safety pins and sharp shears.

SEWING SUGGESTIONS

Sew with a size 10 or 12 standard machine needle and a stitch length of 10–14 stitches to 1 in. (2.5mm). Use good quality polyester thread. When sewing net as an underskirt use lapped seams (page 128) to avoid unnecessary bulk. On tulle use narrow French seams (see page 124) or hairline seams (see page 125).

Sewer's tips

It is difficult to transfer pattern markings to such open weave fabrics. Rather than using pens, chalk, or tailor's tacks, use safety pins or machine sew tiny darts. This is useful when gathering an edge evenly on a waist or frill.

Fabrics with special properties

Modern fabrics have been developed to give them various properties to satisfy particular needs. These may include water- and showerproof qualities, insulation, extra comfort, or protection against burning. Some of these fabrics will not need any special sewing treatment, but others may need different handling and care.

General advice

- Check the full length of the cloth for flaws before cutting out. It cannot be returned to the store if you discover these after you have started cutting.

- Follow the manufacturer's instructions (if given) to retain any special properties.

- Always test scraps for washing, ironing, cutting, and stitching before starting.

- The special finishes may alter the handle of the fabric, so choose styles wisely.

PVC-backed fabric

Cotton, and other fabrics, are sometimes coated on one side with PVC to make them impermeable and so waterproof.

GARMENTS/PROJECTS

Waterproof coats and jackets, protective aprons, hats, and bags of all sizes.

CUTTING OUT

Use weights or pieces of sticky tape to secure the pattern to the fabric as pins will leave holes, damaging the waterproof quality. Use sharp scissors or a rotary cutter and mat.

SEWING SUGGESTIONS

Use a Mictotex or leather needle in a size appropriate for the weight of the fabric. Use a longer stitch, approximately 8 stitches to 1 in. (3mm). Choose a good quality polyester thread. Attach a walking foot and use plain seams (see page 123) finger pressed open, or push both seam allowances to one side and top stitch through all layers. Seal the seams on the inside with silicone glue or glue tapes over the seams. Glue hems in place to avoid stitching (see page 144). Use an absorbent fabric for lining.

Plastic/vinyl

Plastic or vinyl without a woven backing lacks durability. These fabrics are completely waterproof and—to retain this feature—garment seams must be sealed.

GARMENTS/PROJECTS

Waterproof coats and jackets, hats, protective aprons, and bags. Clear plastic is used for panels in garments.

CUTTING OUT

Use weights or sticky tape to secure the pattern as pins will leave holes, damaging the waterproof quality. Use sharp scissors or a rotary cutter and mat.

SEWING SUGGESTIONS

Use a Microtex or leather needle in a size appropriate for the weight of the vinyl. Use 7 or 8 stitches to 1 in. (3mm), and a good quality polyester thread. Attach a walking foot and use plain seams (see page 123) finger pressed open, or push both seam allowances to one side and top stitch through all layers. Seal the seams on the inside with silicone glue or glue tape over the seams. Glue hems in place to avoid stitching (see page 144). Use an absorbent fabric to line garments.

Felt

A bonded or felted fabric is produced direct from fibers that are matted together, rather than woven or knitted.

GARMENT/PROJECT

Crafts and toys; bags and coats.

CUTTING OUT

As there is no grain, the fabric pieces can be cut out in any direction so less fabric is required. If there is no obvious right side, then choose a side and be consistent when cutting out (chalk a cross on the wrong side). Use shears for cutting.

SEWING SUGGESTIONS

As the fabric is often quite thick, use a standard size 14 machine needle and lengthen the stitch slightly to about 8 stitches to 1 in. (3mm). Choose a good quality polyester thread and use plain seams pressed flat, or top stitch the seam allowances to one side to reduce bulk.

Showerproof fabric

Fabric which is showerproof will resist a bit of rain but cannot be described as fully waterproof.

GARMENTS/PROJECTS

Shower curtains, lightweight coats, jackets, and ponchos.

CUTTING OUT

Use weights to secure the paper pattern to the fabric as pins will leave holes. Use sharp scissors or a rotary cutter and mat.

SEWING SUGGESTIONS

Use a size 10 Microtex needle and about 8 stitches to 1 in. (3mm), as fewer holes will weaken the fabric less. Use a good quality polyester thread which will not rot or weaken with wetting. Use plain seams with both seam allowances pushed to one side, and top stitch through all layers. It is not necessary to seal the seams as the fabric is not designed for waterproof garments.

Ripstop nylon

Ripstop nylon is a woven nylon fabric with reinforcement threads across the warp and weft to strengthen the cloth and prevent it ripping. It is a very strong, lightweight, windproof fabric which can also be made waterproof.

GARMENTS/PROJECTS

Jackets and overpants; kites, hot-air balloons, tents, sleeping bags, and flags.

CUTTING OUT

Tends to slip and move, so cutting in a single layer will be more accurate. Use weights rather than pins and cut with sharp shears.

SEWING SUGGESTIONS

Sew with a size 10 Microtex machine needle and about 10 stitches to 1 in. (2.5mm). Sew seams with a serger (see page 66) or use French seams (see page 124, or plain seams (see page 123), with both raw edges zigzagged together (see page 53). A walking foot (see page 19) will help to guide the fabric layers under the needle evenly.

Neoprene
(WETSUIT FABRIC)

Neoprene is a synthetic rubber. It is breathable and waterproof with good insulating qualities. It is often laminated with other fabrics to better suit its purpose, or combined with spandex, in the case of Superflex, and used for modern wetsuits.

GARMENTS/PROJECTS

Wetsuits and waders.

CUTTING OUT

Due to the thickness of the fabric, cut the pattern pieces in a single layer with long-bladed sharp scissors.

SEWING SUGGESTIONS

If possible, use flatlocked seams sewn with a serger (see pages 67–8). If not, use a stretch stitch (see page 55) or narrow zigzag (see page 53). Use a Microtex needle (size 11 or 12) and nylon thread. A walking foot (see page 19) will handle the stretch and the thickness of the fabric easily.

Flameproof fabric

A fabric which has been treated to make it flameproof or flame-retardant will not burn after the ignition source has been removed, or the burning will be delayed. These fabrics must be cleaned and cared for according to the manufacturer's instructions to retain their qualities.

GARMENTS/PROJECTS

Must be used for draperies and furniture coverings in public buildings such as stores, theaters, offices, and schools. Individual homes need not adhere to the same strict guidelines. If you are unsure of the legal requirements please check before starting a project.

CUTTING OUT

Lay flat and cut with sharp scissors.

SEWING SUGGESTIONS

Choose a strong standard needle of around size 14 depending on the thickness of the cloth. Sew with 8–10 stitches to 1 in. (2.5mm). Follow any additional guidelines offered when buying the fabric, otherwise sew as for a similar weight of untreated fabric.

Interfacings

These are designed for use under the fabric of a garment to add body or stiffness to a particular area. They can be sewn in or fused to the wrong side of the fabric or facing.

GARMENTS/PROJECTS

Use interfacings to give body to a front band or collar, or to support areas behind pockets and buttonholes.

CUTTING OUT

Pin the pattern pieces to a double layer of interfacing and cut with sharp scissors. If the interfacing is fusible cut it ¼ in. (0.6cm) smaller to prevent it fusing to the iron or ironing board.

SEWING SUGGESTIONS

If hand sewing the interfacing in place, use a fine needle and silk thread as this is less likely to knot. If heat-fusing the interfacing, place it glue-side down onto the wrong side of the fabric. Hover the iron closely over the interfacing with steam. When the interfacing has settled, use light pressure, then a little more pressure with the weight of the iron to fuse the interfacing to the fabric.

Stabilizers

Blackout lining

These are used to support fabric for machine embroidery to give a better finish. They come with "cutaway," "tearaway," or "washaway" properties.

Blackout fabric is not black in color but generally comes in neutral shades. It is used to line drapes to exclude light and noise, and can also help with insulation.

GARMENTS/PROJECTS

Use a stabilizer on the wrong side of the fabric when embroidering a motif or design on a shirt, sweatshirt, skirt, dress, or jacket. Use to support lightweight and sheer fabric when sewing a row of pre-programmed stitches.

CUTTING OUT

Cut a piece larger than the design.

SEWING SUGGESTIONS

Use a machine embroidery needle and good quality thread for the design. Select the appropriate stabilizer for the type of stitching and the weight and structure of the cloth. Follow the manufacturer's instructions for best results.

GARMENTS/PROJECTS

Separate linings and for lining plain drapes and shades. (However, it is quite stiff and does not hang well.)

CUTTING OUT

Measure accurately and cut with long-bladed sharp scissors for a neat edge.

SEWING SUGGESTIONS

Machining will leave tiny holes in the blackout fabric which may let light through. If this is a problem, glue the fabric panels together. To sew seams use a standard size 9 needle and 8–10 stitches to 1 in. (2.5mm). Sew plain seams but push the raw edges to one side and top stitch through all layers. This will keep them flat. Blackout fabric is better when made up as a separate lining, as it can be too stiff as a sewn-in lining.

Leather, suede, and their faux alternatives

In recent years textile technology has seen the development of fake furs, leather, and suede which closely resemble their natural alternatives. In addition, these are often much easier to sew and care for than the "real thing."

General advice

- Choose styles wisely and make a muslin first to check the fit. Mistakes can be costly or impossible to rectify, especially when working with animal fur.

- Cut fur and fake fur from the wrong side with a blade or needlework scissors. Do not cut the fur pile.

- Keep styles simple with a minimum of seams.

- Machine natural skins with a leather needle and use a Microtex needle for synthetics.

- Be aware that an ordinary domestic sewing machine may not be able to sew thick and heavy leather and fur.

Leather

The skin of an animal, leather varies in size, weight, and texture, and is dyed and finished in different ways.

GARMENTS/PROJECTS

Cowhide for coats, pants, jackets; smaller skins for bags, belts, hats, and slippers; lambskin for skirts and dresses; upholstery.

CUTTING OUT

Use the spine as a grain line and place pattern pieces, held down with weights. Dampen leather with a sponge and cut with a craft knife with a protective mat below. Thinner leather can be cut with sharp shears.

SEWING SUGGESTIONS

Use staples or small bulldog clips for seams. Hand sew with a leather needle. Use a suitably sized leather machine needle and 8 stitches to 1 in. (3mm). Sew with polyester or buttonhole thread. Attach a walking foot and sew plain seams (see page 123). Finger press the seams open and glue the raw edges to the wrong side of the fabric. Use rubber-cement glue for hems (see page 144) and hold in place with a heavy book until set.

Faux leather

Faux leather is often a vinyl-coated fabric with color and surface texture similar to leather. It can be produced in a decent length rather than having to work with a number of small natural skins.

GARMENTS/PROJECTS

Coats and jackets, pants, bags, hats, belts, and furnishings.

CUTTING OUT

If thin enough, sharp scissors can be used. For thicker weights use a craft knife and protective mat on the table below. Use weights to attach pattern pieces.

SEWING SUGGESTIONS

Use a standard or leather needle in a size appropriate for the weight of the fabric. Sew with approximately 8 stitches to 1 in. (3mm), as fewer holes will weaken the fabric less. Choose a good quality polyester thread. Attach a walking foot and use plain seams (see page 123) finger pressed open, or push both seam allowances to one side and top stitch through all layers. Glue hems (see page 144) in place or fold up and top stitch.

Suede

Suede is an animal skin but—unlike leather—is the inside layer of a cowhide, pigskin, or lambskin, with a napped finish.

GARMENTS/PROJECTS

Coats, jackets, skirts, pants; bags, hats, belts, slippers.

CUTTING OUT

Use the backbone as a guide for the nap and cut all pieces in the same direction. Use sharp shears for lightweight suede and a craft knife for heavier weights. Use weights rather than pins to hold the paper pattern in place.

SEWING SUGGESTIONS

Use staples or bulldog clips to hold fabric together. Use a suitably sized leather machine needle and 8 stitches to 1 in. (3mm). Sew with polyester top stitch or buttonhole thread. Attach a walking foot and sew plain seams (see page 123) to join fabric pieces. Finger press the seams open and glue the raw edges back to the wrong side of the fabric or top stitch to one side. Use rubber-cement glue for hems (see page 144) and hold in place with a heavy book until set.

Faux suede

Synthetic or faux suede has been improving over recent years and some are remarkably realistic. They are easy to wash and care for, and do not ravel or crease. There are also many woven or knitted fabrics with a brushed surface that have the appearance of suede and are easy to sew.

GARMENTS/PROJECTS

Coats, jackets, skirts, pants; bags, hats, belts, slippers.

CUTTING OUT

Place all pattern pieces in the same direction. Use weights rather than pins to hold the paper pattern in place and cut with sharp shears.

SEWING SUGGESTIONS

Sew with a Microtex machine needle and 8–10 stitches to 1 in. (2.5mm). Use good quality polyester thread and sew mock flat-fell seams (see page 126) to join fabric pieces. Attach a walking foot for best results. Fold up hems and top stitch to finish.

Fur and faux fur

faux
fur

real fur

Fur is seldom worn today and faux
alternatives of most popular types are
readily available.

GARMENTS/PROJECTS

Simply styled coats and jackets with few
seams; cuffs and collars; cushions and throws.

CUTTING OUT

Real fur should be cut from the wrong side with
a craft knife. Cut fur fabric with sharp, short-bladed
needlework scissors through the backing. Try not to cut
the pile. Cut all pieces in the same direction without a
seam allowance.

SEWING SUGGESTIONS

For faux fur sew with a standard needle (size 12) and
polyester thread. Place the fur sides together and
machine zigzag stitch (see page 53) over the raw edges.
This will allow the seam to lie flat and should not trap
any pile. Use a leather needle for real fur and construct
seams in the same way but stabilize them with twill
tape. Use false or faced hems (see pages 138–9). Line
garments with a luxurious satin lining.

Sewer's tips

Keep the vacuum cleaner close
at hand when working with fur
fabric as the loose fibers get
everywhere! Cutting from the
wrong side with needlework
scissors can help slightly.

Fabric preparation

Manufacturers helpfully provide us with cloth that is ready to use. However, it is usually a good idea to prepare the fabric to remove any unwanted residue and help prevent shrinkage in the completed garment.

Methods of pre-shrinking

The following pre-shrinking methods are provided as a guideline only. If in any doubt, cut a piece of fabric from the length and test it first.

STEAMING

For delicate fabric, hover the iron half an inch above it and slowly steam the entire length. Lay it flat to dry off (hanging it off the edge of the ironing board or up to dry can stretch and distort it). A tank iron (see page 13) has a good supply and pressure of steam, which makes this process easier.

This method of pre-shrinking is suitable for fabrics made from wool and silk fibers, and velvet and velveteen (with the wrong side uppermost). Loosely woven fabrics should also be steamed, as washing may cause the weave to shrink and crinkle, changing the texture of the cloth.

Finished garments should be dry cleaned to retain the best look.

Tweed, camel, cashmere, mohair, bouclé, organza, dupion, Thai silk, georgette, velvet, and velveteen are suitable for steaming.

HAND WASHING

Hand washing with a gentle detergent, or none at all, can pre-shrink some fabrics. The fabric should then be spun with no heat and laid flat to rest and dry (again, hanging to dry can distort and stretch). It may then need to be pulled straight and ironed flat before being cut out. Hand washing will also remove any residue that might cause slipped stitches when machining.

This method is suitable for cotton and cotton-blended fabrics, and for knitted and lace-structured fabrics, such as Slinky Knit and hand-knitted fabrics. Faux leather, suede, and fur fabric should be treated this way, and then dried at a cool temperature in a tumble dryer.

The completed garments may be hand washed and possibly washed by machine.

Voile, lawn, batiste, corduroy, and chenille are just some of the fabrics that can be hand washed to pre-shrink.

Harder-wearing fabrics such as denim and jersey will benefit from a machine wash prior to sewing.

NO TREATMENT

Pre-shrinking is not always suitable: dry-clean garments; beaded and sequin-covered fabrics; satins and silks for bridal wear; and leather, fur, and suede should not be pre-shrunk. Canvas, upholstery fabric, PVC (vinyl), Neoprene, and ripstop nylon do not need to be pre-shrunk either.

MACHINE WASHING

More tolerant fabrics can be machine washed on a warm, delicate cycle (with a gentle detergent) to pre-shrink them. They can be dried in a warm drier (not hot) before they are cut out. Washing this way may improve the handle of some fabrics, softening them and making them easier to sew.

Use this method for denim, cotton shirting and sheeting, microfiber, linen, and hemp fabrics. Jersey, including sweatshirt and T-shirt fabrics, must be pre-shrunk this way. Note that some strong-colored fabrics may lose their color through machine washing.

Finished garments with fabric pre-shrunk this way can be machine-washed.

DRY CLEANING

Some fabrics may benefit from dry cleaning prior to sewing up if the other treatments are unsuitable.

Not all fabrics need to be pre-shrunk—consult the manufacturer's guidelines if in doubt.

Laundry care

To prolong the life of garments once they are made, clean only when necessary and by the most appropriate method. Over-washing in a machine at a high temperature will wear out garments all too quickly—the color will fade and the surface texture of the cloth will become distressed.

DRY CLEAN

Dry clean bridal and evening wear made with delicate fabrics and/or with any construction built in to retain the look and structure (boning, interfacings, and canvas).

Jackets, coats, and suits should be dry cleaned so that they keep their shape.

Dry clean specialist fabrics (that require a delicate treatment) with a suitable chemical.

Bridal wear and evening dresses are often dry clean only due to decorative touches.

HAND WASH

Lingerie, lace fabrics, woolens, and garments made from delicate fabrics should be washed gently by hand. Some may need to be dried flat, while others will need to be spun (slowly) to remove most of the water.

MACHINE WASH

Most garments can be machine washed, but care should be taken to choose the lowest possible temperature required and the most delicate cycle for the fabric. Turn garments inside out to protect the surface of the cloth. Synthetic fibers will not require as long a spin or as hot a drying temperature as cotton or linen. If you are unsure, check the care label on a similar bought garment before washing for the first time.

IRONING

To ease the task of ironing, fold garments carefully when dry or arrange them on hangers to prevent any extra creases forming. Some garments may not need to be ironed at all. Iron from the wrong side or use a muslin or silk organza pressing cloth to protect the surface if necessary.

WASHING SILK FABRICS

Immerse the fabric in a solution of warm water and mild, pure detergent. Rinse in clean water and allow to air dry.

Press using a warm iron to straighten the grain of the fabric. Do this before attempting any stitching.

Fabric care symbols

Hand washing	Machine washing	Bleaching	Pressing	Dry cleaning
	86°F 30°C			
Do not wash by hand or machine	Machine washable in warm water at stated temperature	Bleaching not permitted	Do not press	Do not dry clean
	86°F 30°C			A
Hand washable in warm water at stated temperature	Machine washable in warm water at stated temperature, cool rinse, and short spin	Bleaching permitted (with chlorine)	Press with a cool iron	May be dry cleaned with all solutions
	104°F 40°C			P
	Machine washable in warm water at stated temperature, short spin		Press with a warm iron	May be dry cleaned with perchlorethylene or fluorocarbon or petroleum-based solvents
				F
			Press with a hot iron	May be dry cleaned with fluorocarbon or petroleum-based solvents only

Glossary

BIAS
The diagonal direction of fabric between the warp and the weft threads.

CALENDERING
A finishing process which uses steam and rollers over the surface of cloth to polish it.

FABRIC
The result of yarns having been woven or knitted together. In some cases, fibers are felted or bonded direct into fabric.

FIBER
A single natural or synthetic "hair" which is then spun with others into a yarn.

FINGER PRESSING
When using an iron is not appropriate fingers can push fabric into place.

JACQUARD
A type of loom which can create intricate designs through operating the threads independently.

LAYERING
When trimming raw edges to limit bulk on the inside, trim each layer to a different height.

MERCERIZATION
A treatment applied to cotton to give it strength and luster.

MUSLIN
A test or mock-up of a garment made in a cheap cloth; also referred to as a "toile."

NAP
A surface texture on a cloth which makes it appear different from different angles. Pattern pieces must be cut in the same direction on a napped fabric.

NOTIONS
The items required to complete a garment or project, including zippers, buttons, elastic, etc.

PILE

Extra fibers or loops which have been woven or knitted into a fabric during manufacture, e.g., velvet or toweling.

PILLING

Through wear, small balls of fiber can appear on the surface of some synthetic fabrics. They can be picked or cut off.

PVC

Poly Vinyl Chloride, sometimes called vinyl.

SATIN WEAVE

Many floating threads lie over the surface of a satin cloth to reflect light and give it a shine.

SEAM ALLOWANCE

The distance between the stitching line and the edge of the fabric when sewing pieces together. A standard ⅝ in. (1.5 cm) is often used.

SELVAGE

The finished edges of a cloth which do not ravel.

SHEARS

Long-bladed scissors for cutting fabric.

SIZE

A stiffening added to fabric to give it bulk. It is often washed out.

TWILL WEAVE

A weave with an obvious diagonal rib on the surface.

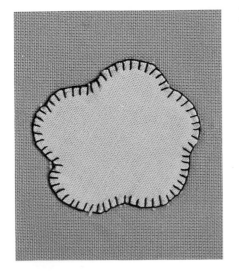

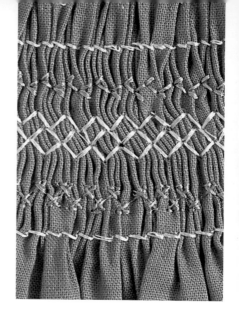

UNDER STITCH

When the seam allowances are stitched to the wrong side of a garment and the stitching is not seen on the right side, e.g., on trouser side-pockets.

WARP

This refers to the threads put on the loom first before a fabric is woven. The weft threads are then woven between.

WEFT

The threads making up the filling yarns of a woven cloth.

WITHOUT NAP

A fabric without a napped surface does not have to have all its pattern pieces cut in the same direction.

WOOLY NYLON/FLOSS THREAD

A bulked thread used on sergers to give a decorative finish to a seam.

WORSTED

Worsted wool fabric has had its yarn combed first so that the fibers lie smoothly in one direction.

YARN

Made from fibers that are spun together.

Resources

Magazines

Altered Couture
www.stampington.com/html/altered_courture.html

Butterick
www.butterick.com

McCall's
www.mccall.com

Sewing Savvy
www.clotildessewingsavvy.com

Sew Stylish
www.taunton.com

Sew News
www.sewnews.com

Sew Today
www.sewtoday.co.uk

Sewing World
www.sewingworldmagazine.com

Threads
www.taunton.com/threads

Vogue Patterns
www.voguepatterns.com

Websites

Sewing machine companies:
www.brother.com
www.elna.com
www.husqvarnaviking.com
www.janome.com
www.berninausa.com
www.babylock.com
www.pfaff.com
www.singer.com

Others:
www.sewingpatterns.com
Patterns from the most popular pattern companies on sale online.

www.isew.co.uk
Hints and tips, and news of events.

www.sewing.org
Non-profit organization with the aim to get people sewing.

besewstylish.taunton.com
Online resource and sew blogs.

www.madeiraus.com
Information about threads and stabilizers and where to buy them.

Index

Credits

I would like to thank the following for their help in the search for fabric samples for the Textile Directory: Stone Fabrics, Ambassador Textiles Ltd., Elite Fashion Fabrics, Second Skin, The Curtain Factory Outlet, John Lewis, Whaleys (Bradford) Ltd., The Hemp Store, and Dress Fabrics for Elegance.

Thank you to Brother UK for supplying the sewing machines on which all the machine samples were sewn, and for the feet illustrated on pages 18 and 19.

Thanks to Terry Fox for her insights into the world of couture sewing and her basic format for categorizing fabrics.

Quarto would like to thank the following for supplying material for use in this book:

Makower UK
118 Greys Road
Henley-on-Thames
Oxon RG9 1QW
Tel: +44 (0)1491 579727
www.makoweruk.com
Email: info@makoweruk.com

John Kaldor Fabricmaker UK Ltd
www.johnkaldor.co.uk
Email: info@johnkaldor.co.uk

James Hare Silks
PO Box 72
Monarch House
Queen Street
Leeds LS1 1LX
Tel: +44 (0)113 243 1204
Fax: +44 (0)113 234 7648
www.jamesharesilks.co.uk
Email: sales@jamesharesilks.co.uk

MacCulloch and Wallis Ltd
25-26 Dering Street
London W1S 1AT
www.macculloch-wallis.co.uk